FRIENDSHIP WITH GOD

David Hope was born in Wakefield in 1940 and educated at Nottingham and Oxford Universities. He later continued his studies in Bucharest. He was ordained in 1965 and served as a curate in Liverpool and a vicar in Warrington. From 1974 he was Principal of St Stephen's House, Oxford, then in 1982 became Vicar of All Saints, Margaret Street, London. In 1985 he was appointed Bishop of Wakefield.

THE ARCHBISHOP OF CANTERBURY'S LENT BOOKS

*Previous titles available
from Fount Paperbacks*

The Way of a Disciple
George Appleton

Prayer and the Pursuit of Happiness
Richard Harries

The Way of the Cross
Richard Holloway

Gethsemane
Martin Israel

Looking Before and After
Helen Oppenheimer

Be Still and Know
Michael Ramsey

Seeking God
Esther de Waal

FRIENDSHIP WITH GOD

David Hope

With a Foreword by
the Archbishop of Canterbury

Collins
FOUNT PAPERBACKS
in association with Faith Press

First published in Great Britain by Fount Paperbacks, London
in 1989 in association with Faith Press

Printed and bound in Great Britain by
William Collins Sons & Co. Ltd,
Glasgow

CONTENTS

FOREWORD BY THE ARCHBISHOP
OF CANTERBURY   7

1 The Call to Repentance   9
2 Back to Basics   22
3 Into the Wilderness   36
4 Childlikeness   50
5 Martyrdom   65
6 Transfiguration   79
7 Waiting for the Risen Christ   93

FOREWORD

by the Archbishop of Canterbury

I once knew a man who said he made it part of his Lenten rule to read the Archbishop of Canterbury's Lent Book "no matter how painful the experience". Were he still alive, he would find this book sheer pleasure. This is not because David Hope is dismissive of some of the more rigorous elements of Lenten discipline. He recognizes the value of well-ordered Christian discipleship but this book is no doleful Lenten list of fasts and duties. It is alive with the sense of God and his capacity to break through into our lives. It is good news.

This book has been written by a working Bishop amongst the countless other demands of episcopal office. Perhaps this is why there is much sanctified commonsense in its pages. Doubt is not dodged, but neither is God's capacity to overcome human weakness denied. David Hope finds his illustrations often in the Holy Land and its places, and in the holy people of past Christian centuries, those places and people whom God has touched. He shows how friendship with that God who touches his world comes as a gift to transform and redeem us. Lent is a good time to renew our determination to receive that gift with humility and joy. This book will be a sure aid to all who seek to do so.

Robert Canterbury.

FRIENDSHIP
WITH GOD

1

The Call to Repentance

On any reading of the gospels there is a striking urgency and immediacy in the call by Jesus to the first disciples. This urgency is reflected in Mark's narrative of the call of Simon and Andrew (Mark 1:16-20). Jesus says to them, "Follow me and I will make you become fishers of men." The response comes – "and immediately they left their nets and followed him". The use of the word "immediately" is no doubt in part to be attributed to Mark's own style, yet his use of it in this way throws up for us in sharp relief the fact that Simon and Andrew, "left their father Zebedee in the boat with the hired servants and followed him".

The response to Jesus has indeed been immediate; with it there has been a complete change in their way of life. Nothing is secure, nothing is promised for the future. Again, in the famous account of Paul's "conversion" the writer of the Acts of the Apostles presents the reader with a similar event. Paul is on his way and nearing Damascus, "breathing threats and murder against the disciples of of Lord" when "suddenly" a light from heaven flashes about him and he is confronted by the Lord.

Here is the authoritative and often quoted passage (the *locus classicus*) for all who claim such a sudden and dramatic conversion experience to the living Lord. There are very many testimonies down the Christian ages, from very many individuals, to the way in which the Gospel message has struck them in an instant, and their lives have been changed. Augustine, sitting in the garden with his friend, lights on the words from St Paul's letter to the Romans (13:13-14) ... "Not in rioting and drunkenness, not in chambering and wantonness, not in strife and envying: but put ye on the Lord Jesus Christ; and make not provision for the flesh, to fulfill the lusts thereof." Quite literally this is how Augustine himself describes this amazing conversion moment ... "No further would I read; nor needed I. For instantly even with the end of this sentence, by a light as it were of confidence now darted into my heart, all the darkness of doubting vanished away."

Another similar event is instanced in the way St Antony hears the answer Jesus gives to the rich man who comes to him asking the question "Teacher, what good deed must I do to have eternal life?" (Matthew 19:16-22). "If you would be perfect, go, sell what you possess and give to the poor, and you will have treasure in heaven; and come follow me", was the uncompromising response of Jesus. Unlike the rich man with great possessions in the gospel narrative, who went away sorrowful, Athanasius tells us of Antony ... "He went into the church pondering these things, and just then it happened that the Gospel was being read, and he heard the Lord saying to the rich man, If you would be perfect, go, sell what you possess and give to the poor, and you will have treasure in heaven. ... Immediately Antony went out from the Lord's house and gave to the townspeople the possessions he had from his forebears ... and selling all the rest that was portable, when he collected sufficient money, he donated it to the poor, keeping a few things for his sister."

Antony became the father of that prophetic protest movement which flourished in the Egyptian desert in the fourth century; this set out in an uncompromising way that dimension, as its members saw it, of the Gospel call which demanded of them nothing less than everything. Such a response has persisted in individuals and groups, notably in the religious orders of the Church and those in various ways associated with them; it is a positive commitment to simplicity, poverty, and chastity.

Such a turning to embrace a wholly new way of life, a sign that the individual has indeed responded to the call to repentance and to the new life offered in Jesus Christ, is reflected in the event of Christian initiation. For as a prelude to the actual dipping in the water there is what is now called in the Church of England service "The Decision". In earlier times it was described as "the renunciation" (*apotaxis*) of the devil and all his works, and the Commitment (*apotaxis*) to Christ, the adherence or adhesion to Christ in the profession of faith. (The two parts which comprise the Decision of the Anglican Alternative Service Book (A.S.B.) Baptism/Confirmation service reflect this older usage, in that the candidate having been asked that key question – "Do you turn to Christ?" – and having given the response "I turn to Christ", is then asked about the renunciation of sin and the rejection of evil.)

It is only then that the questions concerning Christian belief in God – Father, Son and Holy Spirit – are put as an integral part of the baptism itself. The renunciation of Satan is described vividly by Cyril of Jerusalem (c.315-86): "You first entered into the vestibule of the baptistry, and, while you stood and faced the west, you were told to stretch out your hand. Then you renounced Satan as if he were present, saying: I renounce you, Satan, and all your pomp and all your worship." Theodore of Mopsuestia speaks of a similar action and similar words: "Once more you are standing on hair cloth with bare feet, you have taken off your outer garment and your hands are stretched out to God in the attitude of prayer. Then you kneel but you hold your body upright. And you say: I renounce Satan and all his angels, and all his works, and all his worship, and all his vanity, and all worldly error; and I bind myself by vow to be baptized in the name of the Father, of the Son and of the Holy Spirit."

These renunciations were consistently made with the candidate or candidates facing west, and Cyril explains why – "I will explain to you why you stand facing the west. As the west is the region of visible darkness, and since Satan, who has darkness for his portion, has his empire in the darkness, so when you turn symbolically toward the west, you renounce this dark and obscure tyrant." Once the renunciation had been accomplished in this fashion, the way was then open for the candidate to complete the process by the profession of faith. In order to do this, a turn was made from west to east, a deliberate act for the one now entering upon the Christian profession, the way of Christian discipleship. This is the turning of one's back upon the powers of darkness to face in the opposite direction. Again, Cyril of Jerusalem has both description and explanation: "When you have renounced Satan and broken the old pact with Hades, then the paradise of God opens before you, the paradise which he planted in the east from which our first father was driven out because of his disobedience. The symbol of this is that you turn from the west to the east, which is the region of light, so you are told to say: I believe in the Father, and in the Son, and in the Holy Spirit, and in one baptism of penance." St Ambrose, in describing the baptismal rite in Milan, mentions precisely this same movement: "You would turn to the east. For the one who renounces the demon turns himself to Christ. He sees Christ face to face."

This orientation to the east has remained embedded in the Christian tradition. Many of our churches are built on an east/west axis; even now some people make a deliberate turn toward the east, if they are not already doing so, as they recite the Creed, for precisely the same reasons as are adduced by Cyril and Ambrose. In ancient times, in places of prayer and in private houses, a simple cross could be found painted on the east wall of a room, suggesting that Christians prayed facing east. There is certainly evidence that at the point of martyrdom or indeed death, the custom was to turn east. It is narrated in "the Passion" of Perpetua that she saw four angels who were to carry her to the east after her death. And it is recorded of Macrina, sister of St Basil, who "at the moment of her death, was conversing with her heavenly bridegroom", that she did not cease to fix her eyes on him, "for her bed was turned towards the east". Prayer to the east appears to designate Christianity, in contrast with prayers towards Jerusalem for the

Jews, and later on towards Mecca for the Muslims, an important distinction in the three great monotheistic religions (see Jean Daniélou, *The Bible and Liturgy*, 1966).

In this way then, "the Decision" prefigures both symbolically and verbally what was to happen in the descent into the baptismal waters. Indeed, very often the actual profession of faith was made in the water itself, the candidate being dipped each of the three times at the mention of the names of the Trinity – Father, Son and Holy Spirit. St Paul in his letter to the Romans (6:3-11) spells out the fact that all who have been baptized have been baptized into Christ Jesus. We have been baptized into his death and resurrection . . . "we have been buried with him by baptism into death, so that as Christ was raised from the dead by the glory of the Father, we too might walk in newness of life." The baptismal waters are at one and the same time both destructive and creative. It is death-dealing and life-giving water, and in passing through the water the candidate moves from death to life, in communion with Christ.

That same movement is evident in contemporary services of baptism, now severely shorn of much of the ancient ritual and symbol. The long, and in some places very long, period of preparation for initiation into the Christian family and fellowship, the involvement in the process itself – stripped naked as a sign of our original state,

15

going down into the water and coming up again on the other side to be clothed in the white robe of the redeemed, being led with thanksgiving and rejoicing into the waiting company of believers, there to celebrate the Lord's resurrection – such a process must have left an indelible memory. Having been signed with the sign of the cross, it was with you for the rest of your life, however that life happened to turn out for the future. There could be no doubt about the force of this sacramental action in the life of the individual concerned.

In the early church the season of Lent came to have an important place in the whole process of initiation. Baptisms were only performed once, as a rule, in the whole Christian year, and that was at Easter. However long a time of preparation had preceded baptism, Lent – the last five weeks before the actual ceremonies themselves during the night of Easter – was an opportunity finally to refresh, rehearse and reinforce the content of the instruction which had gone before. Not unnaturally other members of the Christian family came to share in this process with those coming freshly to an exploration of the faith. The content of the instruction varied from place to place; (certainly in Jerusalem) it continued for some time after the baptisms at Easter, so that those most closely guarded secrets of the Christian mysteries on Baptism and the Eucharist were only shared by those who were actually baptized. But many Christians of long standing took the opportunity to refresh and renew their own understanding of their faith during the Lenten period. Lent groups are not altogether a modern invention!

Every Christian comes to experience sooner or later a kind of dulling sensation in regard to their faith. That original enthusiasm, that original blinding light which drew one to Christ, and more clearly and deeply towards and into the life of the Church, goes dead and faith no longer seems to have that excitement about it that once it did. There are those, too, who would not recognize this aspect of turning to Christ, the experience of instant conversion or the blinding light in their lives. Rather they would wish to affirm a somewhat more hesitant and altogether more halting process at work, drawing them into faith. For there are those who appear to continue utterly convinced, bold and firm in their affirmation, whilst others find they stumble much more along the way of unknowing. Yet all would still wish to speak of "commitment" to Christ, whilst acknowledging that there are moments, sometimes longer periods, of real and serious questioning, of deep doubt, times when we perceive within ourselves that the edge has gone from our discipleship, when it would appear that we have gone back on that to which we so proudly gave ourselves in our baptism. This particular aspect of Christian experience we shall be exploring in greater detail in a later chapter.

We can perhaps best comprehend the implications of baptism for us in the continuing living out of our Christian discipleship. For this was the reason for those rites and ceremonies surrounding the service of baptism. They were not simply decorative additions; they were there, the stripping, the anointings, the turning from west to east, all these symbolic actions, both to spell out and draw out more clearly for the initiant and also for those who had already been baptized, the many aspects and implications of the central event, the immersion in the water.

But whilst baptism itself may certainly be described as an "event", baptism is also a "process". We grow into our baptism. That baptismal process is traditionally completed at confirmation, when with our own hearts and our own lips, we take on for ourselves our baptismal promises and commitment, making the decision for Christ of our own free and unfettered will.

That process goes on. When as an early teenager I was confirmed, I thought something dramatic would happen to me. I'm not quite sure what I expected, but I did expect that God would, almost overnight, change me for the better. The service itself was an occasion to remember: a Friday night in early December, when I knelt before the then Bishop with my twin sister – in the same place and in the same cathedral in which I now myself administer the sacrament as Bishop – determined to be good! That couldn't and didn't last, because I had got it all wrong. The Christian religion isn't about being good, it is about being holy, and being holy has nothing to do with being pious. It has much more to do with becoming or being the person God created and wants us to be, of "growing up in every way, into him who is the head, into Christ" (Ephesians 4:15). So whilst acknowledging that original event of baptism/confirmation, that moment of conversion to which one can authentically testify, the experience which changed one's life for Christ – however one may wish to speak of how or what it was that led you to Christian discipleship – there is still the business of living that out here and now today, and the fact that today is part of that process of living and growing in Christ which was celebrated and proclaimed in that once-upon-a-time event of incorporation into Christ in baptism. The Decision made then, the renunciation of Satan and the adherence to Christ, the dying with and in Christ and the rising to new life in him, continues both as "then" and "now"; that movement from death to life into which we have already been drawn continues to draw us onwards and forwards and to inform our living this and every day.

The title for this chapter is taken from the introductory words to be used by the celebrant at what is described as "An Order for the Beginning of Lent".[1] The introduction to the service reminds all Christians that by a careful keeping of the days of Lent they might "take to heart the call to repentance and the assurance of forgiveness proclaimed in the Gospel, and so grow in faith and in devotion of our Lord". The message of Jesus, and his call to those who would follow him, is concerned with repentance. This repentance, this change of heart of which the Gospel speaks, is not just or only a once and for all event. Involved in the very word repentance is the whole process of movement and change. In proclaiming that the time was fulfilled and the Kingdom of God was at hand, Jesus said "Repent, and believe in the Gospel". For the Christian disciple, in the enterprise of daily seeking to live out the demands of the Gospel, there has always been that tension between, as St Paul puts it, "not doing the good I want but the evil I do not want" (Romans 7:19), or in the words of the Book of Common Prayer, again echoing St Paul, "having done those things which we ought not to have done and having left undone those things which we ought to have done". We have to be aware that even in spite of our best endeavours, even though we strive to open ourselves the more to

[1] From the collection of services and prayers entitled "Lent, Holy Week and Easter" commended by the House of Bishops of the Church of England, and published with their agreement.

God's transforming power and love, we fall short in many and varied ways; to put it bluntly, we sin. However the sin might be explained or we might wish to explain it away to ourselves, the sin and the sinner cannot be so easily separated; finally we need to own the fact that we have all sinned and fallen short of the glory of God. Nevertheless we are justified by his grace as a gift, through the redemption which is in Christ Jesus (Romans 3:23-24).

Even after the long and arduous business of preparing for baptism, after the impressive ceremonies associated with this sacramental incorporation into Christ, the fact that individuals could and did sin grievously gave rise to much debate in the early Church as to whether it was even possible to re-admit to the Christian fellowship any who had so transgressed and fallen away. Although there was a hard core of those who could not accept that re-admittance was possible, or even if it was, it could only be granted once in a lifetime, it came to be accepted early on that provided an appropriate penance was served for such failure (the penance was public and often prolonged) then re-admittance was a possibility. The contemporary church is not over concerned with sin, unless sexual misdemeanours are concerned, but the fact remains that, left to ourselves and our own instincts and affections, we do easily and so readily go astray.

The call to repentance then is a timely call, for

it forms a continuing dimension of our claim to Christian discipleship. It means, further, that some action on our part is needed, decisive and urgent action in response to that generous invitation which God in Christ sets before us. Repentance is about the putting off of the old and putting on of the new, about life in the Spirit – life in Christ, rather than life without the light and grace which we have come to find in him. The call to repentance has been interpreted as a call to life-long penance. This was so in times past; and there may be those who would urge such a view at the present time, but the Christian response is not negative. In responding to this call of Christ we are locked in to a movement and process which continues throughout our lives, which needs to be earthed day by day, and in which, if we are truly and whole-heartedly to embrace the following of Jesus Christ, inevitably there will be a conflict of priorities and interests. However, if the controlling vision of our discipleship is that generosity of heart and life which comes from the freedom and joy which we have in Christ whilst we are yet sinners, then the call to repentance which the Lord sets before us in the context of his Church each Lent will be a refreshing opportunity to each of us to allow him to enter our lives more fully, in the power of his Spirit. We can then let go of ourselves into the transforming power of that love which only he can perfect in us.

Questions for Discussion

1. What does Jesus' call "follow me" mean for you today?

2. What does it mean when we pray that we may "grow into" our baptism?

3. How would you explain the meaning of dying and rising with Christ in baptism?

2

— ✠ —

Back to Basics

We saw in the previous chapter how Lent became associated with the final period of preparation for those to be brought into membership of the Church, and how other Christians had come to use this as an opportunity to refresh and renew their own understanding of the Christian faith. In very many churches Christians today use the season of Lent as a similar opportunity to explore together their common faith and the way in which their living out of that faith impinges on the many and varied circumstances of life in the world. The original principle still operates, for in this season we can renew more deeply the love and knowledge of Jesus Christ which had once captured our imagination and caught our vision. I still receive the magazine from the parish in which I served my curacy in Liverpool; and in it a scheme for regular Bible reading through Lent, and suggestions for a Lent Rule, is divided helpfully into three sections – 1. Prayer and Worship, 2. Fasting and Self-Discipline, 3. Almsgiving and Service. These provide an outline for the "basics" with which this chapter is to be concerned. But first of all we must look at the phrase "Lent Rule".

A Lent Rule used to be a vital part of the keeping of Lent. Those three Sundays, quaintly called Septuagesima, Sexagesima and Quinquagesima, before the onset of Ash Wednesday, gave ample warning that Lent was approaching. The Gospel for Quinquagesima Sunday sets the scene with a passage from St Luke in which Jesus tells his disciples – "Behold we go up to Jerusalem . . . ", so the direction and destination of Lent is firmly fixed in Jerusalem and what is there to be accomplished through the death and resurrection of Jesus.

This is the context in which the Lent Rule is to be conceived and lived. In times past ideas were adopted which seem somewhat petty now – no sugar in tea, no cakes on Fridays, no cooked breakfasts in Lent. Yet such small gestures did have a point and continue so to do. Of particular note was the regular saving of money each week to put into a Lent Box, and which would go to some worthy object, either for the local church or for the church abroad. These schemes continue today. But the Lent Rule, like any rule of life, whilst it might comprise a number of items, nevertheless needs always to be conceived as a total entity – a framework, guidelines within which we move forward on this particular part of the Christian pilgrimage. Different situations and circumstances alter the emphasis of such a rule from year to year, but it is a Rule and not rules and regulations of which we are speaking. It is the basic ground plan on how to approach these five weeks, of particular significance to the Christian Church, and in which we are encouraged to intensify our priorities towards God in order that the roots of our faith may be deeper and stronger, and our living out of that faith in the contemporary world may be the more confident.

It is important that we have this framework, some pointers for the way ahead and forward, so that we can be more truly and fully freed. Without it, we so easily lose our way and find ourselves overwhelmed by the immediacy of the next thing to be done or responded to. Some rule of life, some Lent Rule is of positive value as we attempt to get our priorities right, and ensure that balance for real living which takes a proper account of who and what we are, and the needs of body, mind and spirit. Not least it reminds us that we are not simply tied and bound to the things of the moment, that there is that dimension to us as human beings which needs to be nurtured, that aspect of every person which might be described as "soul". Here I speak not of soul as opposed to body, but of that which is within every human being; the deep mysterious elements of affection and emotion, of mood and temperament, of relationship and solitude and loneliness, of aesthetics and wonder and appreciation – all that side of us which can be trampled down almost to the point of extinction by the unremitting materialism and pursuit of our own selfish ends which so characterizes the times in which we live.

If we are to remain truly human, we need to be helped to stop and to look and to listen, to be receptive and reflective – so our rule for life, more especially our rule for Lent, will enable us to recover something which we were in danger of losing, something which was pushing us in the direction of becoming less than the fully mature human being that God in his infinite love and mercy has created us to be. To think about "being", to assume what Erich Fromm would call our "being" mode, are essential if we are indeed to take seriously the fact that each of us is created in the image and likeness of God. How we distort and deface that image which should be reflecting something of God's glory! The aim and object therefore in any rule for life will not be the further to restrict and restrain, but rather to release and free our best energies to become more human. Inevitably the guidelines that we set for ourselves, usually in consultation with an experienced and mature Christian, a spiritual director as sometimes that person may be called, may seem to be somewhat irksome and cumbersome. But like learning to drive a car with regularity in practice the whole exercise becomes much less threatening and gradually you are no longer overwhelmed by the mechanics of it all, until it comes quite naturally and you are free to enjoy it. Such is the aim of a rule for life or a Lent Rule.

I would like now to look more closely at the three particular aspects of what a Lent Rule might comprise.

PRAYER AND WORSHIP

Prayer and worship are a necessary part of any Christian life, so why mention this as a particular feature for Lent? Basic though they are we do need the opportunity to take stock of them on the regular basis which Lent itself provides. For the idea of any Lent Rule is not that it should be in any way distinct and apart from what applies during the rest of the year, but rather that it should focus on aspects of the Christian life which ordinarily we tend to take for granted, and which then begin to disappear from view. [A Lent Rule has been described as enabling us to do the more ordinary things extraordinarily well!] There will be those who perhaps need some encouragement in their worship, who need organised and practical help in going to church and sharing in public worship on a more regular basis, and in a more committed way. For there should be a commitment on the part of every Christian believer to being with the rest of the Christian community as it gathers for worship Sunday by Sunday to celebrate regularly God's mighty act in raising Jesus from the dead. From the very beginning this has characterized Christian discipleship, and the celebration of the Eucharist has typified in all manner of circumstances that belonging which we have in Christ with the whole Church on earth and in heaven. For the Christian, Sunday is the start of the week and not the end of it. Sunday is the day which gathers up what has been experienced and lived during the past week, set out before the Lord as we bring before him ourselves, our souls and bodies, to be re-invigorated and strengthened by our sharing in the communion of the Lord's body and blood sacramentally given; and then sent out once more into his world ourselves, there, in loving and serving him in others, to give as richly and fully as he has given to us and for us. So Sunday is both completion – fulfilment, and preparation. It has about it that paradoxical quality of being a day of the week, and yet it has an altogether different feel, quite apart from any religious connotations, although clearly stemming from them. Eusebius of Alexandria, writing in the fifth century, draws a parallel between the first day of creation and the resurrection which is the first day of the new creation in Christ: "the holy day of Sunday is the commemoration of the Lord. It is the Lord's because he is Lord of all days. It was on this day that the Lord began the first fruits of the creation of the world; and, on the same day, he gave to the world the first fruits of the resurrection. This is why this day is the principle of all doing good; the principle of the creation of the world; the principle

29

of the resurrection; the principle of the week."
Christians, therefore, have a continuing duty to
keep Sunday special. Sunday, starting off the new
week, gives the clue to how it should be for us for
the rest of the week, gives the context in which the
rest of the week should be faced, whatever it may
hold for us.

The public worship in which we join together
is precisely thanksgiving to God for his mighty
act in raising Jesus from the dead. No wonder
the New Testament writings encourage us always
and everywhere to give thanks. Here is the clue to
the thrust of our private prayer also – primarily a
thanksgiving to God. Basically prayer and worship
are about relationship, relationship with God, and
in the power of his Holy Spirit with each other
in the communion of the Church. Ideally there
ought to be resonances of the prayer which we
make together in public, in our private prayer. A
particular verse of Scripture speaks to you as it is
being read during the course of the service, a line
or verse of a hymn strikes you as exactly what
you need to hear just now, verses from the psalms
seem to express much better than you ever could
that feeling of anger and resentment or fear. In all
these instances my advice would be to take away
with you the hymn, the psalm verse, the Scripture
passage or whatever. Recall it quietly and gently
from time to time, as you walk down the street,
as you wait for a train, as you do the washing up

or the cleaning – mull it over, savour it, allow it to go deep, so that it becomes a part of you and your living during the week ahead. There are then many opportunities for our own prayer during the week which may be gleaned from our prayer and worship together Sunday by Sunday. We need therefore to prepare for our worship together, to look ahead expectantly to what the Lord will give to us and share with us as we pray "cleanse the thoughts of our hearts".

There are many books on prayer. It is easy to be distracted into reading so much about prayer, the various ways and methods and techniques, that you never get down to the real discipline of prayer. This involves making some time and space to be still and silent, changing the state of your mind, so that prayer becomes a natural part of your daily life, just like taking a walk, eating, sleeping. The Jewish prayer tradition has its many and various *berakah* forms of prayer – of which this morning prayer is a fine example – "Blessed art thou, O Lord our God, King of the universe, Who hast hallowed us by thy commandments, And commanded us to occupy ourselves with the words of the Torah." Such thanksgiving and prayer, used in different circumstances throughout the day, is not dissimilar from the Celtic, where again prayer punctuates movement from one activity to another in a wholly natural way, as for example in this prayer: "At Fire Lighting" – "As I light this fire, Lord, I bend my knee and lay myself before you. Kindle in my heart a flame of love . . . ." I was reminded of this way of prayer in Tanzania, when I accompanied Bishop Yohana Madinda on what he called his Confirmation Safaris. We were up early and on the road for long distances in order to get to a particular village and church by lunchtime for the service. In the jeep, before ever the ignition was turned on, prayer was offered, very naturally and briefly, for the Lord's protection on our journey. Such journeys can be hazardous indeed! When we reached our destination, a brief prayer of thanksgiving was made. And always before any meal, grace was said. Life was lived out in the context of prayer – it seemed the natural thing to do. Once prayer is divorced from life and becomes a purely pious and individualistic exercise then it runs the risk of becoming totally irrelevant.

We all need times, periods of solitude and withdrawal, when we can develop the art of listening and being receptive to what the Lord God would address to us in the depths of our being. This is a withdrawal which leads those who are prepared to risk themselves into that place where the strife is at its fiercest. Prayer is not something we do, rather it is this ordinary and continuing relationship which we have in Christ, that which we have seen was established sacramentally in the new birth of baptism. Given that daily response as we turn to Christ, it goes on deepening and maturing and growing. Prayer is more a way of life for the Christian disciple. And Lent is the time when on a yearly basis we can ensure that it remains so.

FASTING AND SELF-DISCIPLINE

Fasting and Self-Discipline are not the most immediately attractive features of Lent; yet historically and traditionally both of them have formed part of our Lenten fare. Indeed, prayer and fasting are linked in the New Testament; and the basis of our fast during these forty days is the basis of Lent itself, namely Christ's own experience in the wilderness. The Gospel of Matthew puts it in this very straightforward manner – "Then Jesus was led up by the Spirit to be tempted by the devil. And he fasted forty days and forty nights and afterward he was hungry." In theory the Church still enjoins upon its adherents both fasting and abstinence, even setting out the days and period when such a direction should be observed. Much more acceptable these days are such things as the sponsored slim for Lent, the corporate Friday "fasting" lunch, with the profits given to charity or some third world project.

But the Christian discipline of fasting is more radical than that; it is an attempt to state clearly that men and women, within the freedom with which they are entrusted, do need to exercise a degree of control for themselves, over what they

33

eat and what they drink, and to be able to say no and mean no, lest they become slaves to their worst selves. Involved in the dignity of our humanity is the ability to exercise this discipline. Furthermore, in affirming that triumphal verse in Genesis – "And God saw everything that he had made, and behold it was very good"(Genesis 1:31) – we are not given the liberty of simply ravaging and tearing apart God's good creation for our own satisfaction, for our own greedy ends. Our fasting further reminds us of our interdependence one with another. For in the deliberate act of going without, I am thereby releasing something for someone else. In a world of macroeconomics, such gestures make little apparent impact; yet increasingly Christian people, along with many others, are rightly concerned at the vast imbalance of resources throughout the nations of the world, both of raw materials and of consumables, and the way in which the world's food is so inequitably distributed. So in the act of fasting, the individual is making a deliberate and conscious choice to be with the hungry and the starving, the marginalized and the poor. Such a choice is a word of protest too, which, whilst it may not be heard in the cacophony of the market place, is nevertheless a word which must continue to be spoken on behalf of those who have little or no voice whatsoever with which to plead their cause.

In so far as it is impossible to separate out body, mind and spirit, fasting also has a refining and focusing effect when it is linked more specifically with prayer, as it is in the New Testament and the Church's tradition. There is a sense in which it may be rightly claimed that fasting is a spiritual discipline, the body interacting with mind and spirit in this way, to heighten our awareness of the spiritual. This is far from too unhealthy and too intense a concentration upon fasting alone and as an end itself. The crucial point of any fasting is that it is done within a context, within the spectrum of prayer and worship, almsgiving and service, and as a constituent part of any rule for life.

Fasting has disappeared almost wholly from the programme both of the Church and of the individual Christian. Lent is the time when all of us might both reflect and take some action in this regard, and Friday, the day associated with our Lord's passion, is a good day on which to start a weekly fast. Having established the Friday fast during the course of Lent then it can be continued throughout the year.

ALMSGIVING AND SERVICE

The approach to almsgiving and service is best set out in a passage from St John Chrysostom – "Would you honour the body of Christ? Do not despise his nakedness; do not honour him here in church clothed in silk vestments and then pass him by unclothed and frozen outside. Remember that he who said, 'This is my body', and made good his words, also said, 'You saw me hungry and gave me no food', and, 'in so far as you did it not to one of these, you did it not to me'. In the first sense the body of Christ does not need clothing, but worship from a pure heart. In the second sense it does need clothing and all the care we can give it. . . . Adorn your house if you will, but do not forget your brother in distress. He is a temple of infinitely greater value."

Our Lord encourages us to put our money, our treasure, where our hearts are; the question has to be asked – are our hearts really committed? The view is also held that money is evil, it is dirty, and that Christians should not be concerned with it or about it. But that is not to live in the real world; money *is* a part of the real world in which we live, and therefore is to be used responsibly. As part of this responsible use of money the Gospel encourages us to give to those in need. Further, a quite proper use of our alms is to give as generously as we can to the upkeep and maintenance of the Church, for in so doing we are not only contributing to a building, we are hopefully contributing to a people engaged in telling forth the wonderful works of God and attempting to live out this good news in lives of generosity and service to others. I am constantly amazed by the begrudging nature of those who on the one hand affirm their indebtedness to God who has given them so much and so generously, yet render back to him so little.

"The Lord loves a cheerful giver" is heard in our churches. Yet I have seen few of these cheerful givers! But this is precisely what we need if the Church itself is to be that authentic sign in the world of the costly giving and service which is so much part of the life of Christ and of the gospels. Furthermore, let it not be a drudge but rather a joy as we recall the words of St Francis: "It is in giving that we receive." Here the saint echoes the words of the New Testament; in Acts (20:35) as part of Paul's farewell, it is written "remembering the words of the Lord Jesus, how he said it is more blessed to give than to receive" – and Paul had been called upon to give to the uttermost, to the shedding of his blood for the sake of the Gospel.

In the giving of self in service towards others we become individually caught up in that which must be characteristic of the Church as a whole, its service of Christ in the world. Often in the face of vast human need it seems impossible for the individual to make any significant response, to be able to do anything which is likely to make any difference on a global scale. Yet we have to make a start somewhere and that somewhere is where I am right now. We begin with our own situation, the place and context in which we find ourselves at the present moment. Further, the small, the seemingly insignificant and very ordinary acts of service in which we become involved do begin to address in a very real way that volume of human need and distress which seems so insurmountable. To take on a neighbourhood activity and to become involved in it on a practical basis does satisfy that need within ourselves to be needed, but at the same time can begin to make an enormous difference to the whole quality of life for another person. Many are already involved in such acts of service, many more could become involved. Lent could be the time to start or renew your efforts, looking for a need and taking on what you can reasonably manage.

Very often if we are to move forward then we shall need to take stock of where we have come from and where we are now. This chapter is in no way an encouragement into regression but rather a refining and clarification from the point in our Christian pilgrimage at which we presently find ourselves, to ensure that these very constituents which form the basics of any Christian discipleship are still present in our lifestyle. The fundamental question remains to be responded to day by day – "Do you turn to Christ?" – and if your response continues to be "I turn to Christ", then necessarily the implications of this must needs be wrestled with in the context of today's world.

Questions for Discussion

1. How do you understand the phrase "pray unceasingly"?

2. What part do you think fasting should have in the Christian life?

3. What do you think the attitude of Christians towards money should be?

3

—✠—

Into the Wilderness

In the first chapter we saw that the original enthusiasm with which we turned to Christ can and does wane. It is also a common experience for many that their faith "dies" on them. Writers on prayer and spirituality speak of the onset of times of "darkness" and "aridity". In other words, sooner or later, anyone who sets out along the way of Christian discipleship will find themselves in what the psalmist calls that "barren and dry land where no water is". It is not a pleasant place to be. No longer is it possible to pray, confident in the knowledge that he is there listening; rather, he seems more absent than present. Boredom and disillusionment begin to set in, and you seem helpless to do anything about it. Like certain forms of depression, this comes upon you unexpectedly; you have no idea if and when things are likely to change for the better. These times in Christian discipleship have often been compared with a going into the wilderness, for the description of barrenness, of nothingness, of dryness, has best characterized what is actually being experienced. But the fact that the Lord himself went into the wilderness must be a comfort in our own circumstances; for he himself has been in that place of extremity before and his grace will provide.

Those who may not have experienced such acute feelings, but who yet have been physically present in desert places, may begin to understand how this inner experience feels. One of the particularly memorable parts of my visits to the Holy Land have been journeys to Qumran, alongside the Dead Sea, and further south to Massada. Depending on the time of year, it can be overwhelmingly hot; a kind of blinding white heat beats down upon you – it seems as if you are walking around in an oven. If you can manage to escape from the noise and chatter of your fellow travellers for a while, it is eerily quiet and still, there is no life apart from the insects and lizards darting and scurrying around in the blistering sand and dust. The rocks are cleft and the ground parched. If you wander around on the top of Massada, you must go gently and stop frequently to take a drink to avoid the risk of dehydration and heat exhaustion. So that quaint verse of the Victorian hymn writer does in fact get the mood right –

> Sunbeams scorching all the day;
> Chilly dew drops nightly shed;
> Prowling beasts about thy way;
> Stones thy pillow, earth thy bed.

If the wilderness, the desert experience, were to be summed up in one word, then that word would I think be "absence". It is this "absence" which is articulated by those who feel they have lost their way, that the original joy of faith has gone, that the whole Christian enterprise has something of the barren and arid about it. The outward physical experience of being in a desert place is the best way of describing what is experienced at this stage of the Christian life and pilgrimage.

We can often feel guilty and isolated as we see others apparently not in the least troubled or perturbed by such symptoms. They continue, buoyant and confident, without any sign of the knowledge of darkness and barrenness. The fact is that we are all very different in our responses, and in our experiencing and living out of the Christian life. But we can begin to take courage and confidence from the fact that such experience is not in any way a-typical; rather it is something that we might be led to expect if we are at all to be drawn more deeply and richly into the continuing life of God's people. From the Bible we can gain positive assistance and considerable reassurance both about ourselves and the condition in which we find ourselves. After all, the people of Israel were in precisely the same place. God, it sometimes seemed to them, was a fraud. The narrative of how Israel was led by Moses out of slavery in Egypt, through the waters of the Red Sea, and into the freedom and liberty

of the promised land, is of fundamental significance. All was not well. Having reached the edge
of the Red Sea, it looked as if death would be the
only way out, either at the hands of the Egyptian
hosts, hotly in pursuit, or by plunging into the
water to risk drowning. The Israelites lost their
nerve; they questioned Moses impetuously – "Is
it because there are no graves in Egypt that you
have taken us away to die in this wilderness? What
have you done to us in bringing us out of Egypt?
. . . It would have been better for us to serve the
Egyptians than to die in this wilderness." Undaunt-
ed by these assaults, Moses said to the people, "Fear
not, stand firm and see the salvation of the Lord,
which he will work for you today . . . the Lord
will fight for you, and you have only to be still."
This could be considered foolish advice in view of
the extreme situation in which they found themselves. But [in any case by that stage there was
nothing they could have done that would at all
have alleviated their situation] – the Lord did
indeed fight for them. The people passed through
on dry ground, and their Egyptian pursuers were
swallowed up and destroyed in the Red Sea. But
their trials were not over. Having reached dry land,
the Promised Land, a land overflowing with milk
and honey, life was not what they had expected it
to be. In the long and tedious wanderings which
followed so dramatic an intervention by God for
their deliverance, as time passed the brightness and

43

vividness of their response faded, and murmurings against God took over. They began to look back as they had at the brink of the Red Sea; they would almost have preferred to have been in Egypt in slavery than free and no nearer their destination. The passage from the book of Numbers (11:4-5) sums up well this "looking back" – "Now the rabble that was amongst them had a strong craving; and the people of Israel also wept again and said: oh that we had meat to eat! We remember the fish we ate in Egypt for nothing, the cucumbers, the melons, the leeks, the onions and the garlic, but now our strength is dried up, and there is nothing at all but this manna to look at!" I suspect that many of us can find our feelings reflected in this passage all too well.

This "looking back" creeps into all our lives at some point or another, and with varying degrees of intensity and duration. Given the fact of a present unease, uncertainty, unresolvedness about myself and my own circumstances, it becomes all too easy to look back to the days when everything was all right, when there were no problems and difficulties, a period of contentment and happiness. It probably never was really like that, but from the painfulness and precariousness of the present, the past takes on the glow of that illusory "good time". Paradoxically, this can also take on the form of fantasies about the future; I look forward to the good time ahead when, once delivered from the things that presently oppress me, I can live in my dream home with a newly made fortune and enjoy a life which is trouble free! But again, it can never really be so, because life itself isn't like that. For a variety of reasons there are times, periods when the going seems to be rougher and the pressures tougher; it feels as if your nerve is going to break and you won't be able to cope. Maybe at precisely the same time this desert-like aridity is upon you, and the God whom you thought you could count on to bring you through seems nowhere to be found.

Perhaps the real problem is that you are not looking in the right place at all. The escape routes you have explored and found to be empty, the fantasy past and the fantasy future, these have diverted you from looking in the place where you ought not to be surprised to find God – right where you are, in the very thick of it, and with you in the present desperate moment. The very place you had not expected to find him, the very place you had never thought to search, this present moment which you would rather escape and flee – you find God is here right now. Further, instead of searching to find him here or there, you discover his presence within. So often we need to hear those words of Moses, when we panic, when we are at our wits' end – "Fear not, stand firm and see the salvation of the Lord which he will work for you today . . . ".

There are within the Christian spiritual tradition those who have drawn our attention to the present moment; in the writings of Jean Pierre de Caussade, especially in *Self-Abandonment to Divine Providence*,* again and again he calls us to recognize and really to live in this present moment – so present to him is this time that he speaks of it as a "sacrament" – a gift from God, this here and now, a moment so freely and lovingly squandered by God, a moment pregnant with his will, his activity deep within, towards me and all around me. De Caussade writes, "We must confine ourselves to this present moment without taking any thought for the one before or the one to come." He is not saying anything which our Lord himself did not say when he enjoined those who would be his faithful followers to take no thought for the morrow. In an even more contemporary vein, Michel Quoist reminds us that, "Throughout the course of daily life we are to make use of the opportunities offered to take a new hold on ourselves and to welcome God into our lives." He continues – "While you are waiting for the bus, or for your motor to warm up, or for your supper to cook, or for the milk to boil, or for your coffee to cool off, or for a free telephone kiosk, or for the traffic lights to change . . . don't kill time: no matter how short it is, it can be a moment of grace. The Lord is there, and he is

*Also published as *The Sacrament of the Present Moment*

inviting you to reflection and decision."

Those of us who are entrusted with ministry within Christ's Church are sharply reminded every day of our lives of the here and now of this "today", in the words of the opening psalm (the Venite) at Morning Prayer – "Today if you will hear his voice . . . " a stern summons that it is in this "today" of my life that I am called to respond fully and generously to the demands which the Lord makes of me, and not to be deflected or captivated by the various escape routes of yesterday or tomorrow, always so attractive, but which in the end we find to be a dead end.

Another aspect of the wilderness, the desert experience which I mentioned in passing in connection with a visit to the Holy Land, was the almost eerie silence about those waste places, away from the crowd. In the Christian tradition the desert has come to be symbolic of that silent, listening, waiting aspect of Christian prayer. In the first chapter we noted the immediate and totally uncompromising response of Antony as he heard the Gospel account of the rich young man being read. He chose quite deliberately to go into the silence and solitude of the desert, and there to gather round him others of like mind, who were ready quite literally to forsake all and make their way apart into a desert place. The Desert Fathers, and indeed the Desert Mothers, lived out a protest, as they saw it, to the far too comfortable accommodation that the Christian Church had made towards the state of the world. Here were holy zealots and holy fools who were prepared to go to extreme lengths because they cared desperately that the cutting edge of the Gospel would become so softened and blunted that it would no longer have the converting power to change the world. A remarkable collection of stories and sayings have emanated from the desert. From these, born of the silence of those waste places, and containing elements which can seem bizarre, deep truths about ourselves and our relationships with one another and with God are told to us. The following two extracts, on the subject of silence, are very typical:

I have often repented of having spoken, Arsenius said, but never of having remained silent.

One day Archibishop Theophilus came to the desert to visit Abba Pambo. But Abba Pambo did not speak to him. When the brethren finally said to Pambo: "Father, say something to the Archibishop that he may be edified", he replied, "If he is not edified by my silence, he will not be edified by my speech."

Much of what they are saying may be caught in the phrase "Know yourself". For so often the root cause of our listlessness, the frustration and lostness which we experience in our wilderness state, is the result of a failure to embrace and understand ourselves. Often we have never made the time or had the space to feel really comfortable with the selves we know ourselves to be. Silence and solitude will help us to do just that – to be, to relax and be still, to centre down into our deepest selves and there discover God's abiding presence in us and with us. We are envious of others we meet – "If only I were like such and such a person . . . , if only I had her looks . . . his personality"; all the time we are unconsciously rejecting more and more of ourselves until we become almost convinced of our own uselessness and nothingness. But we have to reach this down and out situation before God can gently and quietly begin his real work of affirmation and reassurance. We have been casting around for so long in our search for him. In solitude and in silence we can better find him; and find our true selves. Being alone and being silent can be very threatening in a society where noise and company seem almost to be a necessity. Yet unless we are prepared to embark on the times of quiet, and to make a regular provision for this in our rule for living, unless we are ready to take the risk, our potential for maturity and for spiritual development will go unfulfilled. Increasingly people are finding the need to make a retreat, to take some positive action in their inner growth. There are places and people who are specially to help, who gladly and warmly welcome those who come to recognize this need within themselves. It may seem to be a very daunting step to take, to enter into a world of silence for even a day, let alone a whole weekend or a week. The reward only comes when you have actually made the move and experienced the quality of such silence, which Kierkegaard describes as the "homeliness of eternity". And it is in this context also that more naturally we are able to take to ourselves the advice of another of the Desert Fathers, Isaac the Syrian, who suggests, "Enter eagerly into the treasure-house that lies within you, and so you will see the treasure-house of heaven: for the two are the same, and there is but one single entry to them both. . . . Dive into yourself and in your soul you will discover the rungs by which to ascend."

A quiet day or retreat weekend offers solitude and sets us on the right path. But we need to extend this, to find a place for solitude and quiet within the ordinariness of living. Make the most therefore of the time and space that you have to yourself and for yourself, and don't feel guilty about so doing. Keep an eye out in the daily routine for those few brief moments when you can come to the surface for air, so to speak, when you can sit back, if only momentarily, when you are able briefly to disengage from that which is pressing in upon you – work, or family or life generally. Make a special time for peaceful meditation, if you can. One of the best ways to achieve this new space is to make a deliberate effort at some point in the week to get out for a walk. You will feel better for it, and you will return to the struggles and problems of the day in a more relaxed and refreshed way, enabling you to tackle them not only the more confidently but also the more satisfactorily.

"The ordinariness of living" was for the Israelites the desert place – the scorching sun, the unrelieved view of vast sandy wastes, the tedious and meagre provisions. Our circumstances are different, but one day is very much the same as another. Yet, whilst our days may indeed be very predictable with their sloth or their hyper-activity, in the job we do or haven't got, in youth or in old age, married or single – each day does bring its own quality and flavour, and no matter how our days may seem, there are highlights which make the rest of it seem liveable. Nevertheless, most of us would describe our mode of existence as ordinary. But we are not sufficiently alert and alive to the fact that in the "ordinary" routine God is present. In all typical daily situations and circumstances prayer is possible. All the great religious traditions of the world, and certainly the Christian tradition itself, regard prayer at the beginning of the day as of particular significance. Karl Rahner comments, "Prayer in everyday life is a prayer of fidelity and reliability. It is a prayer of unselfish, even apparently unrewarded service of God. It is the consecration by which the grey hours become bright and the little moments great."

Alexander Solzhenitsyn records in *Cancer Ward* the moment when Oleg is set free from the hospital in which he has been for so long – "He walked on to the porch and stood still. He breathed in. It was young air, still and undisturbed. He looked out at the world – it was new and turning green. . . . It was the morning of creation. The world had been created anew for one reason only, to be given back to Oleg. 'Go out and live!' it seemed to say."

So it is with each new day for each of us. Here is a gift from God which holds out immense opportunities for us. It is the first day of the rest of our lives; whatever yesterday was like, today is wholly new and the future lies ahead. A brief prayer of thanksgiving at the beginning of the day is the least we can do in the hurry which first thing in the morning is for most of us. There are many opportunities for making this commendation to God of yourself and your day in the context of thanksgiving and blessing; incorporate them as part of your morning rituals of washing and dressing. Often this will be the kind of prayer which can easily be recalled in the depths of one's heart – for example, from St Patrick's Breastplate – "Christ be with me, Christ within me, Christ beside me", etc. Equally appropriate is that fine morning hymn of Charles Wesley – "Christ whose glory fills the skies . . . " well known by heart surely to many of us. This will set the tone for the rest of the day, and set this new day in that context with which we begin the whole week as we come together with the rest of the Christian community in thanksgiving and praise to God. The public prayer is assimilated into the private and becomes a part of the whole of life, where God most assuredly is. For the New Testament clearly indicates that this is precisely the place where God is active. So often we look for the special and the spectacular. It was in an out of the way place called Bethlehem, not of any particular note worldwide, that God's Messiah was born. Jesus himself, in his ministry of healing, is often said to have taken the individual "aside", "apart from the crowd". The wonder and the miracle is that God is daily among us and beside us, he has promised to be with us to the close of the age, and so he is. You may often find yourself experiencing God's nearness and presence, not in fact in church, not in that house group or prayer group or fellowship group where you might have expected him to be, but as you are pushing your way through a busy shop, walking down your local street, driving along a road you have driven along many times before, when, if only momentarily, something seems to be different. Suddenly you are aware of his intense nearness to you and closeness with you. Thank him, praise him and go on your way rejoicing.

The desert, the wilderness, is part of everyone's experience in attempting to follow faithfully in the way of Christ. It is not extraordinary, nor is it something which comes to only a few. Generally at some time or another, and for a longer period rather than a short spell, we find ourselves in this wilderness, and our steadfastness and constancy begin to waver. We are sorely tempted to throw in our hand, to abandon the whole enterprise. At its worst the experience can be disabling; more usually it is reflected in a general feeling of depression with ourselves and with the fact that our faith seems dead to us, and what once was a real joy is more now a drudge and a chore. However, this condition should be viewed, not so much as a problem but as an opportunity for growth and for change. It is bound to feel uncomfortable, even painful, but it is a further stage along that way to which we responded in that Decision long ago – "I turn to Christ" – the full implications of which are only now reaching us. We are learning all over again what it is to be a follower of the Lord in precisely the place from which we have excluded him – the reality of life here and now.

Questions for Discussion

1. How important do you consider it to make spaces and to enjoy silence as a regular part of your life style?

2. How far has the desert impinged on your life thus far? What positive things have emerged from that?

3. In what ways do you experience God's presence in the ordinary routine things of today?

4

— ✠ —

Childlikeness

One of the ways in which in the gospels we are encouraged to see our discipleship, our friendship with God, is as little children. We are not being called to childishness, but to childlikeness. Children must have have been as much a part of daily life in Our Lord's home town of Capernaum as they are of the life of any community at any time. In Matthew 18:1-4 it is in response to a question put to him by his disciples about status – "Who is to be the greatest in the kingdom of heaven?" – that Jesus takes up a particular child, one of a number who no doubt would have been thronging around him as he went from place to place. He doesn't answer the question just like that – having taken the child he then proceeds to tell them that unless they become like this child they will not enter the Kingdom of heaven. So what is it that Jesus finds so attractive in children that he urges upon his followers, those who would be his friends, the qualities of childlikeness?

The first noticeable thing about children is their

insatiable inquisitiveness. What about this? . . . .
Why that? . . . . and those difficult questions like
"Where did I come from?"

The child is captivated by the world into which
he or she has been born: new vistas open out,
each day is filled with exciting and fresh possibilities. What I mean is very well illustrated in that
charming book *Mister God, This is Anna*, where
something as basic and as throwaway as a broken
off stump of an iron railing becomes for Anna such
an object of wonder and mystery . . . "She was
saddened because of the others, the grown ups –
they just couldn't see the beauty of that broken iron
stump – the colour, the crystalline shapes. And she
wanted them to join with her in this exciting new
world, but they could not imagine themselves to
be so small that this jagged fracture could become
a world of mountains, an iron plane with crystal
trees. It was a new world to explore, a world of
the imagination, a world where few people would
or could follow her. In this broken off stump is a
whole realm of possibilities to be explored and to
be enjoyed."

The child searches, the child also questions. He
or she wants to know more, and the very asking
of questions, the searching, is in no way a threat
to them – rather it is exciting, for it is life. The
answers which mother or father, or anyone else,
may give, often seem nonsensical, but that doesn't
seem to matter either. There is exploration and there

is discovery – learning to walk and learning to talk.

The first question which we ought to ask as we continue through Lent and reflect on the theme of childlikeness, should be about this insatiable inquisitiveness in relation to ourselves, to our Christian living and believing – to the enterprise upon which we are all engaged, that search for God. We must look for the courage to pose the hard questions to ourselves and within ourselves, questions which we feel compelled to ask but to which we shall not necessarily find an answer. Are we ready to continue in our Christian discipleship in "the unknowing" rather than "the knowing" mode – to venture more deeply into that struggling and wrestling which any real engagement with God will necessarily involve? Here, it is a healthy reminder which the Eastern spiritual tradition is constantly setting before us, that faith proceeds as much by unknowing as it does by knowing, and that on the whole we want to know too much! But we must still maintain that spirit of insatiable inquisitiveness about our Christian discipleship and living, our longing to know God better. In the older baptismal liturgy, this longing was described as the candidates were led towards the waters of baptism to the words of Psalm 42 – "Like as the hart desireth the water brooks, so longeth my soul unto thee O God: my soul is athirst for God, yea even for the living God: when shall I come to appear before the presence of God?"

It was the rite of initiation which set out the basic pattern of how the Christian commitment was to be lived out day by day for the future. It wasn't a matter primarily of finding God; all the emphasis in this psalm is on thirst and questing, desire and longing for God, for the living God. It is this deep desire and longing which needs to be kept alive in our hearts. It is the same attitude of mind of which the gospel narratives remind us when they set out the "parable" of the pearl of great price, of the searching for the lost coin – there is action, even frenzied action, in the alacrity and zeal with which the search is taken up – the search which is first God's searching out of us, but which must become an insatiable inquisitiveness in us as we go forward in the faith with the same questing curiosity.

Whilst in baptism and in confirmation a statement of the faith we confess is made, our belief, which is the faith of the Church, is publicly and firmly proclaimed in the form of the Creed. Indeed it was from the baptismal interrogation that what is now referred to as the Apostles' Creed gained its more formal and stylized structure, shape and content. But having made our statement of faith as we joyfully and enthusiastically embrace the way of Jesus Christ, we cannot be content simply with the subscription to certain statements of belief enshrined in whatever creed. For faith is not surely a form of words, indeed can never be reduced to a form of words only: faith is relationship, active, alive, deepening and growing, and is very much reflected in those words of Psalm 42. Perhaps those of us who do tend to recite the words of the Creed without thought, Sunday by Sunday, might use the season of Lent to examine more deeply and more carefully both the meaning and the implication of the statements to which we subscribe, and how they actually impinge on the way we fashion and order our lives. As our friendship with God deepens and matures, his friendship with us and ours with him, this will surely begin to have an effect upon the personal ordering of our lives, the way in which our relationships with others are conducted and expressed – even to the deepest relationship of husband and wife – relationships within the family and household generally, and more widely still with the whole circle of people with whom we come into contact. Are we prepared to give others the benefit of the doubt? Are we always ready to think the best of a person, or are we only too ready to notice the negative? What about attitudes to money and wealth, and the many good things of God's creation? Faith and morality cannot be separated either, so as we begin to take more seriously the implications of the Son of God becoming flesh, his taking on of our humanity, then the Church and church members cannot escape an involvement in the social and political issues of the time. To escape into a world of purely spiritual or doctrinal Christianity is to empty the Christian Gospel of meaning. These implications, however, have to be worked out afresh in every age and by every age; not by inventing a new Gospel, but by taking that which has already been given in the Scriptures, and "making the truth of Christ known in succeeding generations".

Mention has already been made of the words "struggle" and "wrestle" in respect of our commitment to faith. These are not new words or ideas, for that original turning from east to west, that renunciation of the devil and all his works and the turning full face to Christ, whilst sacramentally celebrated and accomplished, remains still to be realized in our living out of that turning, day by day. We should not be surprised that we are locked into combat. Many spiritual writers have used these terms to describe the open warfare of the spirit at the very deepest levels of being. The baptismal formulae themselves encourage us to think of ourselves as having been enlisted on the Lord's side to "fight against" all that is evil and wrong, as indeed we have. There are reflections of this view in many popular hymns – "Fight the Good Fight", for instance, as well as in the more familiar exhortation in the Book of Common Prayer that we should pray for "the whole state of Christ's Church militant here on earth". These references are not only to the taking up of arms for Jesus Christ, fighting to make the Good News known. There remains for each of us and within us an element of conflict between the decision we have made for Christ and the way we experience the life of faith as it unfolds through our own lives. But our Lord never promised us an easy time, and his own experience in Gethsemane and on Calvary focus his own experience of fearful conflict and God-forsakenness. The agony of mind and heart are great indeed as he wrestles with the implications of his unswerving obedience to the Father. If there is within us that aspect of insatiable inquisitiveness in our thirst for God, that desire to be obedient to his will, then we also are likely to find ourselves at the sometimes bewildering and painful point of unknowing as we are drawn more deeply into the mystery of God himself. But we must keep up the search and we must keep on asking the questions.

Another feature of our children is that they are so transparently and obviously themselves. There is often mischief afoot, sometimes downright badness – but at least they are open about it! They have their moods and tantrums too, as they burst with rage and scream and kick: they are aggressive and passionate. But as you and I may have the occasional – or even more than the occasional – regression into the infantile, as we grow up and grow older we begin to take on our various poses and disguises, play our subtle, sometimes manipulative games – sometimes consciously and deliberately, sometimes quite unconsciously, unaware that we are so doing. Somehow or another, we attract the encrustations of sophistication – who I am, what I am, becomes blurred. There's a certain tension between who I know myself to be and who another person perceives me to be, even allows me to be, and I don't always feel as free as I might to be myself. There is after all a quite proper concern for and about myself. The Lord commands us "to love the Lord our God and our neighbour as ourselves".

It is this loving of ourselves as we really are which we find so difficult, and which we spend a good deal of time attempting to evade. This quest seems not quite right; there is something about it which seems to go against all that is said about the service of others and love of neighbour. And yet the measure of our love for God and our neighbour is the degree to which we love ourselves. Teresa of Avila has written, "However foolish and useless I may seem to be, I will never cease to praise you, O my God, for having made me just as I am." How many of us can with confidence affirm these sentiments, giving thanks to God for his having made us just what we are? It is this which lies at the heart of our eucharistic thanksgiving as we come before him just as we are – "poor, wretched, blind, tossed about with many a conflict, many a doubt" – as we lay our lives before him for the healing and transforming touch of his love. This self love is not an overindulgent narcissism, indeed it is neither narcissism nor a narrow introspection, it is much more a matter of the way in which we allow ourselves to become the unique and special and beautiful people God created us to be.

There is about children a certain naïvety and innocence which very soon become tainted and are replaced by a calculated cunning! Some of us are very good at putting on airs and graces, some of us hardly recognize that we are putting them on at all. Our difficulty can be simply to be ourselves. The same goes for our prayer. Often we find ourselves resorting to prayer which is not really "us" or "me". If there is a real and deep friendship with God beginning to develop, then let it be so; the whole point about friends is that they don't need to talk at each other the whole time, that once the friendship has started to grow (and that will require work), then it is possible to be together silently and quietly. Such friendship does mean that we are gradually able to become more fully ourselves, to reveal more of and about ourselves in the company of the one we come to know ever more deeply and trust more fully. Again, in the words we use to express our thoughts and ideas, there will be an informality – they will be our words, our phrases, and not someone else's.

This is our own private prayer. There is a huge treasury of public prayer, of the prayer of the Church, of liturgical prayer, of the more formal and solemn prayer which has stood the test of time and which has nourished and encouraged very many souls in their Christian pilgrimage. We may often find ourselves using these prayers in a variety of situations and circumstances, and in our own private prayers. They can and do say very often just what needs to be said from the depths of our own heart and from our present experience of life. On the other hand, there are times when such prayers seem too formal, and where perhaps something more direct, straightforward and informal is more appropriate. And it is here that I find children's prayers extremely helpful. I carry with me a copy of a collection of prayers by children and for children, collected together in the International Year of the Child. Whenever I preach on a particular theme – thanksgiving, for example – it is often the prayer of a child which comes to my aid. One goes like this – "Thank you Lord for the dinner ladies that cook so well and the sheep that keep us very warm when it is very cold and thank you for cows that give us milk so we can drink it . . . and thank you very much for my teacher that tells me a very lot of sums and that makes me very clever. Amen."

Thanksgiving must surely be one of the major themes of our daily response to God. There's a life and a vitality about that child's prayer and an immediacy which at once strikes you as having come direct from the heart. Yes, perhaps it does bring a smile to our faces, but what is wrong with that in a prayer of thanksgiving to God? There are many other prayers in this same book;

the following is a poignant and moving example of the kind which we associate with childhood: "Dear God our Father, please help all the people on the kidney machines to live. Please help more people to donate money so that more research can be done on kidney diseases, and please bless all kidney donors who give life after they die." Here is a prayer of intercession, and its contents will not come strangely to our ears, for surely all of us have prayed this kind of prayer from those very earliest days when we ask God to send us an electric train or a doll or lots of sweets and other goodies, to the point at which we made an anguished prayer with a heavy heart for the sick, the dying, the despairing and the lost, more especially when one of our own family or someone close to us has been in this kind of need. After all, our Lord has quite clearly stated (Matthew 7:7): "Ask and it shall be given unto you, seek and you will find, knock and it will be opened unto you. For everyone who asks receives and he who seeks finds and to him who knocks it will be opened." Yes, we do know this; we follow this advice closely and clearly, we do ask but it is not given; we do seek, but we do not find; we knock and it is not opened to us. So why do we continue asking day after day, week after week – asking, knocking, seeking? We usually make this kind of prayer – intercession, supplication – first for it seems to have a simplicity and directness that an ordinary Christian believer can manage. But here is an area of unknowing, of paradox, of deep mystery where we are drawn into a much deeper and perhaps much more difficult, dangerous, and altogether more risky relationship with God than we had ever anticipated, where it is not possible for us to find all the answers directly given. There is no way to evade some of the deep and real theological issues which intercessory prayer raises: this is not the opportunity for me to explore these fully, but I can suggest one or two lines of approach which may lead to fuller understanding.

One picture I would like to put before you is that in St Mark's Gospel, chapter 2 verses 1-12, the account of the paralysed man carried to Jesus by four friends. They could not get near the house where Jesus was "because of the crowd", but, in no way daunted, still determined in their efforts, they go up onto the roof and let the man down through an opening, laying the paralytic at the feet of Jesus. Several points arise from this narrative. You will have noted the determination, the persistence, of those who had brought the sick man – they are in no way deterred by the first obstacle – the great crowd and commotion they encounter. Secondly, notice the fact that the sick man whom they bring does not even know what is happening to him, where he is being taken, to whom he is being led – he had never so much as heard of the name of this Jesus. The third point to note is that it is the faith, belief and commitment of the four who brought the paralysed man to Jesus – *their* faith, not that of the paralysed man, and the persistence born of their faith – which avails with the Lord on this man's behalf. "They were all amazed and glorified God saying, 'We never saw anything like this.'" From this story we find a very good and helpful approach to intercession – quite simply a laying of the person, the subject matter, whatever, at the feet of Jesus. We are there also, our faith, our persistence and ourselves drawn into the whole process, our very interceding perhaps changing our approach, changing our views, and our ideas. For in our petition, in our prayer, we have been able to see things in a wider and larger perspective; when we set out our prayer may have been, for example, an anguished plea for the life of a dying relative. As time passes that can become an equally anguished prayer for the Lord to take our loved one to himself in joy and in peace. That doesn't always happen, and it is only one example. But it can be so – for we cannot always be sure that our prayer, our desires and hopes and longings for another person or for other people are always or necessarily the best, or right for them. But we do nevertheless bring them to the Lord – we place them in his all-loving, all-sustaining presence, and we must be content to leave them there and to hand them over to him: that is where faith, our own deep trust and confidence in him who has done all things well, must be present. We must always hand over to the

Lord those for whom we would pray, with deepest sincerity.

This leads me on to another example, another way which is given to us by Michel Quoist in his *Prayers of Life*. He presents us with the image of one praying in darkness: the prayer is this – "Lord, I am not alone, I can no longer be alone. I am a crowd, Lord, for men live within me. I have met them, they have come in, they have settled down, they have worried me. They have tormented me, they have devoured me, and I have allowed it, Lord, that they might be nourished and refreshed. I bring them to you too as I come before you. I expose them to you in exposing myself to you. Here I am, here they are, before you Lord." How well this prayer demonstrates that, in spite of our determination to live our own lives in our own way, we cannot escape the fact that, in a whole manner of ways, we are inextricably bound up with many other lives, indeed with the rest of humanity. This is a truth more readily appreciated surely in our contemporary world than ever before. Those things, people and events which already have impinged on my life today thus far – what I have heard on this morning's news, that picture I saw in this morning's paper which disturbed me horribly, the news of a friend's serious illness which arrived in a letter today – these things are those which Michel Quoist says have "devoured and tormented me". You and I bear so much of what we see and hear and read with us and bring it as part of ourselves in our prayer – we can hold them all there before God for his healing, for his restoration. We may find, too, that we are full of anger and resentment against God as we bring some of our more painful and personal concerns before him. It's important for us to feel that we can shake our fists in God's presence at what we consider him to have allowed – or things he has done nothing about. Here, I find verses from the psalms help me to articulate what I can hardly bring myself to say in God's presence – there is a bitterness which I have to get out of my system and which needs to be gathered into and diffused by a realization that this present pain and anger is part of that groaning and travailling of the whole created order as God strives to gather us all into his loving purposes for us.

Another way of approaching intercession which may be helpful comes from a representative of the Society of Friends who writes, "the situation or person may well be in need of our help but we may not know the best way to give it. Perhaps our initial response should be How can I understand? rather than What can I do? . . . " Seen thus the criminal does not cry out to be reformed, the alcoholic to be cured, the atheist to be converted. It is our loving, uncritical acceptance which may be called for in the first instance, undisturbed by our desire to put that person right, to have him or her conform to our notion of desirable behaviour, to "do them good".

We may then be better placed to discover what the most effective action might be and how best we can serve that particular individual.

The prayer which we call intercession, the prayer of asking, the activity of praying for and about other people, circumstances, situations – locally, nationally, internationally – springs from the prayer of a child and leads us into a complex area where our childlike trust in God and of God, where our friendship with him is likely to be put to its severest test. Intercession is an integral part of any act of worship when the Christian family gathers together, just as much as it is an integral part of every Christian's duty to pray for others as well as for ourselves. It is appropriate therefore that we recover during Lent our own commitment to intercession, that we make an effort to remember names and issues and situations, perhaps writing them down, so that before we begin a time of prayer, or as we conclude it, we can slowly allow our eyes and our minds to bring the respective concerns consciously and carefully before God, making the time of prayer on behalf of these as well as for ourselves. Another practical possibility is to reach your church a little before the service, or stay on for a short time afterwards to engage in such prayer. Thus we can bring ourselves and the concerns that weigh in and weigh upon us so heavily, and lay them before the Lord, that his will be done in them and in us "on earth as in heaven".

Questions for Discussion

1. What are the questions about faith which seem to be most prominent just now for you?

2. In what ways can you say you have experienced God both in "knowing" and in "unknowing"?

3. How do you understand Jesus's words "Ask, and it will be given you; seek, and you will find; knock, and it will be opened to you"?

5

— ✠ —

Martyrdom

"The true martyr is he who has become the instrument of God, who has lost his will in the will of God, and who no longer desires anything for himself, not even the glory of being a martyr." Thus speaks Thomas à Becket, in his Christmas 1170 sermon, in T.S. Eliot's *Murder in the Cathedral*. It is a clear and unequivocal statement as to how martyrdom is to be understood, sealed in Thomas's own death as a martyr at the hands of the soldiers who burst into the cathedral and struck him down. Thomas's death is not untypical of the very many down the ages who have suffered, to the point of shedding their blood, for Jesus Christ. Like Thomas, the deaths of many have been sudden and dramatic; for others, martyrdom has been a long, often painful, struggle in prison and captivity, and death may have come as a welcome relief. But for most of us, martyrdom conjures up that dramatic moment in which an individual or group of individuals is done to death for the sake of Christ. We speak in the Christian tradition of the "Church of the Martyrs", of the "age of the martyrs", as we look back to the first beginnings of the Christian faith and its emergence into a pagan and hostile Roman empire. And certainly we can find in the early histories, in the *Acta* of the saints, in the "Lives" of the martyrs (for example, the life of Cyprian, Bishop of Carthage), in contemporary records, very many accounts of those who were done to death in a variety of horrible ways, simply because they refused to acknowledge that there was any god except the God and Father of our Lord Jesus Christ. The liturgical colour red, in use when we celebrate the feast of a martyr, is wholly appropriate, for the blood of which it is both a symbol and a reminder, was the blood not of death but of birth, birth to the life of heaven, the completion and fulfilment of that process begun here on earth, when in their initiation into baptism these martyrs had been grafted into the new life of Christ. Hence we can confidently speak of the celebration of a birthday to heavenly glory. Many names stand out, not least of the apostles themselves – Andrew, Peter, Paul, James and others – from those periods of persecution of the Christians by the Roman emperors, Nero, Decius, Valerian and Diocletian perhaps best known among them. The Church's calendar keeps their deeds ever before us, as on their day each year we pray . . . "that we may endure reproach and persecution, and faithfully bear witness to the name of Jesus Christ our Lord".

It is all too easy, however, to consign the age of the martyrs, the Church of the martyrs, to that past, to that period of time with its gladiatorial contests and amphitheatre sports, which came to a conclusion around the beginning of the fourth century. The term "martyr" has come to mean only this. But as we all must know and recognize, martyrdom did not suddenly cease in the fourth century; in our own times the mention of but two names must serve to remind us that the twentieth century is a century of martyrdom, an age of martyrs just as that past age was. For many Anglicans the vicious death of Archbishop Janani Luwum, during the ghastly period when Amin was President of Uganda, brought home the fact that Christian believing and commitment can still lead to murder and death. Likewise in Central America, the sudden shooting down of Archbishop Oscar Romero in his own church as he celebrated the Eucharist brought shock and sadness to many Roman Catholics and other Christians.

These two deaths only focused what is presently happening in this century of the Church's existence, no more nor less than it did in the first four centuries or indeed in any age – the fact that there are many people in our world who have given their lives unto death for the sake of Jesus Christ and his Gospel. We live in an age of martyrdom; for those of us who live in areas where our profession of faith is not a direct threat to our lives, we should do well to reflect that within the same family and fellowship – that body of believers throughout the world – there are those who face such a possibility daily. They must always have a special priority in our thoughts and prayers, for very often it will be the knowledge that they are being held and sustained in the fellowship of Christian prayer which enables them to keep faith. The more that we can put aside the testimony of the martyr as a past phenomenon of Christian faith and life, and realize that presence among us now, today, the more likely it will be that our own Christian commitment will be strengthened and sharpened. For as we recall and celebrate those who have gone before us in the faith in this way, we discover clues for ourselves and for our own living out of the Gospel.

It is the day of their heavenly birthday that we celebrate, and birthdays are not sad and mournful affairs, they are feasts. That is precisely how the Christian Church has viewed the deaths of the martyrs. In a particular and intense way they have lived out that passage, once upon a time effected sacramentally in their initiation, but later once and for all time, from death to life. Their martyrdom has seen the completion of that process begun in baptism of the individual made one with Christ; they have descended in him into the depths of death and are raised in the glory of the Father, now to share the fullness of his unending risen life. Barbarous and painful deaths give rise to a variety of emotions and responses – but more often than not they have been spoken of by the Christian tradition in terms of victory, victory in and through the mighty power of him who raised Jesus from the dead, and who will also raise our mortal bodies. We may not always be able to rely entirely on every detail of the accounts of such deaths, but we cannot evade the quiet sense of confidence and trust in God which pervades them.

It is in such quiet confidence and trust in God, in the following of Jesus during these days of Lent, that we ourselves need to begin to develop more fully and more deeply – perhaps even to recover altogether. Even if death is unlikely to come to us in the form of execution – in the form of a martyr's death – it is nevertheless clear to us all that "in the midst of life we are in death". Part of living is the preparation for "Sister Death", as St Francis of Assisi calls it, and part of our Lenten discipline is to focus more particularly on how far that sacramental incorporation into the death and resurrection of Jesus continues to be the pattern of our living here and now. Further, we are faced with the question of how far we have been and are prepared to "let go" of ourselves and our own selfishness, our own sinful desires and inordinate affections, in order that the new life of Christ may grow in us. Death marks that final release, whether we like it or not, of ourselves to the One who is the creator and redeemer of all. But already we need to make a more realistic effort for that process of transformation to be more completely effected in us by his grace and love and power.

Thus we are confronted by so much which makes us anxious, fearful, depressed, unable to cope, confused – but these things are capable of being transformed by a quiet sense of confidence and trust in God. At the beginning of the week, as I have looked ahead to what I was supposed to be doing, where I was supposed to be going, I have often found myself asking, "Lord, how on earth am I actually going to make it?" That sense of panic is already present as you wonder just how you are going to get through a particular set of circumstances, a particular week, even a particular day. But then, as we look back, we find that we did actually get through it! But we would have to add, "with God's grace". For if we are able to concentrate more on the present moment and its demands, instead of becoming anxious, neurotic or depressed about tomorrow (which helps neither tomorrow nor today), then we shall survive – and overcome. That is what we hear in the Gospel message of Jesus, and what we see so strikingly in the lives of the martyrs – that singleness of mind and heart and purpose to search for Jesus Christ and to be found by him in the midst of the things of today – our whole mass of experience, some of which is good and some of which is painful and distressing. It is this undeflected fixing of our eyes on Jesus that is

the purpose of our discipleship. In the light of this
we ought not to be reluctant to hand over to him
the many burdens that we bear – this impossible
week, that difficult meeting, even the boredom and
apparent barrenness of one day after another. For
it is these "ordinary" experiences and situations
which are capable of transformation and change,
if only we ourselves are prepared to allow that to
happen.

One of the ways in which this handing over
may be done is in and through our prayer. We
need to make the opportunity to be still and
quiet – bringing the day, the person, the place,
the situation, whatever it may be that is troubling
us, into mind and with the admission "Lord, this is
all too much for me . . . Lord, I am unable to cope
. . . ", as we lay ourselves and the particular set of
circumstances before him. Not least important in
all this is the recognition that – yes, I am unable to
handle this, yes, I do feel inadequate. Allow such
feelings to be verbalized quietly and naturally in
this time of prayer, sustain the silence for as long
as is possible. From this we go forward to become
part of that about which we had been so anxious.
The prayer is no escape into "holy" feelings; rather
it is the very point at which faith and life intersect,
the point at which so often there is an emptiness and
a void, a darkness and an unresolvedness which is
unrelated to the wonder of God. Yet it is precisely
in this darkness and unknowing, as I hand myself

over to the mystery of his love, as I let go of my determination that I am the only one who knows what is best for me, that I begin to discover that his promise to be with me and alongside me and within me always is indeed true. I may not be experiencing that "presence" quite in the way I had expected to, indeed – and paradoxically – it may seem more like "absence", and yet deep down inside, I am able to go forward into the day's events with that quiet sense of confidence and trust in the God who remains faithful to his promises to the end of the day, to the end of the week, yes, even to the end of time.

This is not a panic prayer, not a prayer as a last resort in a moment of desperation when all else seems to have failed, but rather prayer as an ongoing and undergirding aspect of the whole of life, so much so that it is life itself. Far from being a last resort, it becomes the first resort – people, situations and circumstances and the way we approach them and react to them, seem to change radically once we are ready and prepared to lay ourselves and our lives before God in this way. It is a dying to self; a death to arrogance and pride, to our certainty that we know what is the right way for us, an attitude of mind which can only be destructive.

Whilst thus far we have concentrated more particularly on that aspect of the word "martyr" with which it is commonly associated in the Christian tradition, namely one who surrenders his or her life for the sake of Christ and the Gospel, there is also a more fundamental sense in which each and every Christian disciple is called to be a martyr. The root meaning of this Greek word is "witness", and this is an inescapable part of what is involved in becoming a Christian. Every Christian is called to martyrdom, and these comments from Karl Rahner are helpful. He writes: "If we see the prototype of martyrdom as Christ himself, is it not obvious that the martyrdom of our age is far more like his than are those of past epochs? He is the martyr falling to the ground crushed by mortal weakness, the martyr experiencing divine abandonment, hanged between real criminals and scarcely distinguishable from them, the martyr who is almost sure that he is not one, the martyr who can go no further and yet has to go on with the thing that has taken away all his strength, the martyr condemned to the mines for ever – and in our day the mines may not be a place of isolation but simply prison in a land overrun by godless tyranny." The truth is that our initiation into Christ, our becoming members of his Church, is not an introduction into a holy or pious or cosy club. The Christian faith does not promise us an easy and comfortable passage through things temporal until we finally attain to the things eternal. Indeed quite the opposite – if anything we are to expect a rough time! That is spelt out clearly as we are signed with the sign of the cross in baptism:

henceforth we are marked, branded men and women. As we saw in the previous chapter, the Prayer Book use of the word "militant" of the Church here on earth leaves no doubt about the implications of becoming a Christian; and the former vicar of a parish near me here in Wakefield, the Reverend Sabine Baring-Gould, in his popular hymn "Onward Christian Soldiers . . ." indicated that there was to be a militant tendency about the whole enterprise. The commentators on the early rites of Christian initiation refer to the anointing with oil (which was much more of a body rub than the somewhat genteel anointings that take place today!) as something for the Christian akin to the rubbing with oil of the contestants in the gladiatorial games – "You were anointed as Christ's athletes; as about to wrestle in the fight of this world . . ." wrote St Ambrose in his work *On the Sacraments*.

From the very beginning therefore it is spelt out clearly that as followers of him who gave himself up to the death of the cross, we ourselves are now entered upon that same way. The fact that we belong to that family and fellowship of the Church in our local parishes and communities ought to be a great support and encouragement to us, even a great comfort, and a source of real satisfaction and enjoyment. But if this were to become the be all and end all of our belonging, wherein might be the difference between the local church and any other local club or gathering? The words of our Lord himself to us are – "You are my witnesses", and the task is no less threatening and difficult today than it has ever been.

When we bear in mind the association of the forty days of Lent with the beginnings of things, this seems to be an appropriate period of time in which both as individuals and as a local church and community we can reflect upon and sharpen the cutting edge which can so easily and readily become blunted in the sheer complacency of our age, not least in that of the Christian Church itself! This complacency can become all too clear – as when, for example, a local church, during the course of a mission or during a special Lent project, sends out visiting teams in an organized way to visit every house in a given area. Yes, there will be those who simply don't answer the door, and those who will shut the door in your face with a few chosen expletives – but for the most part it is with a shrug of the shoulders and "Not interested" that such visits are answered. I often wonder what we have done to make the Christian faith so dull – surely the most grievous transgression of all! We ought not to be resorting to peddling the Church in this way, as if the Christian faith were on a par with what every door-to-door salesman has to offer. While I recognize the value of these exercises in particular circumstances, and have indeed participated in them myself, it has always seemed to me that the

Church itself ought to compel – by the very quality of its life and the very nature of the relationships of its members one with another, by its worship, and not least by its close involvement in and with the lives of those among whom it is set, in other words by its "witness". For it is this which will attract and draw others magnet-like to its fellowship – the context and the place where they are indeed found by Christ and find themselves in him.

This raises serious questions about the nature of the Church, more particularly the way in which the local church is both seen and experienced by those within, as well as by those without. The church is both buildings and people. The buildings may not be the kind of place which, if we were beginning afresh, we ourselves would choose to construct today. Yet I suspect, however perfect and appropriate any building may seem to be, it can never satisfy all of the people, all of the time. It is possible to speak, however, of a building as having something of a "sacramental" quality about it. As I pass by any church building I ask the question – "Is this building speaking to me of the joy of Jesus Christ who is risen? . . . Is this building speaking to me of life or of death?" And as I make my way through an overgrown churchyard, with rusting half-closed iron gates, towards the church door, firmly bolted and barred, and a noticeboard with the paint peeling off, I cannot escape the conclusion that here is a sign much more of death than of life. The same may be said of a number of acts of worship in which I participate in a variety of churches, where that same sense of deadness, of lifelessness, seems to be communicated. The Christian witness must surely be to a Lord who is risen and who lives; this goes both for buildings and for people.

Any high-street retailer will tell you of the importance, the vital importance, of the shop front, and whether it will entice you in in the first place. I believe the Church has a great deal which we could put in the "shop window", so to speak. There are a wide variety of ways in which the Church, both people and buildings, is making a very significant contribution both spiritual and social to the life of the wider community in which it is set, and without which that local community would quite definitely be gravely impoverished. We are not particularly good at selling ourselves in this respect. Lent is a useful period when, as the local church, we could address ourselves to this task – not just talking about it endlessly, but using the time to evolve a plan of action and carrying it out. Truly churches and places can be transformed when we realize the wider and more practical implications of this word "witness", this call to be martyrs. The whole business of setting our own house in order, of creating an atmosphere in which people will be encouraged to come in and towards the assembled community, will need to be continued and worked at by the worshippers themselves. There is the fundamental ministry of welcoming and hospitality, the development of a sensitivity to the stranger who actually makes it through the doorway – does he or she wish to be smothered in a surfeit of fellowship, or is that person's real need at present to be left to themselves in the surrounds of a warm and welcoming atmosphere? Sometimes our witness is best made when we ourselves are content simply to be. There is too, a tendency among church folk to become cliquish, and therefore for the person on the outside to experience difficulty in easily and readily finding a way in to the heart of the church's life. It has even been known for some more settled and tightly knit congregations not only to be surprised that someone should wish to join them, but to ensure that such a person did not, so great has been the resentment against "new people"! If we are truly to resist these tendencies, if we are to begin to attempt to live out the law of the Lord – to love our neighbour as ourselves; and ourselves to act as we would wish others to act towards us – then more positive action needs always to be taken to make certain that we, as individuals and as Christian congregations, are delivered from such resentment, and from the petty-minded squabbling which can so easily and readily occur among us. Whatever the groups into which we gravitate, it could begin to make a very significant difference within the congregation as a whole if everyone made a determined effort, during the Sundays of Lent, to speak to someone they don't know, someone you have seen often enough and never spoken to, someone even with whom you may have had a row and haven't spoken to from that day to this. Hopefully such a determined effort and exercise on the part of the whole congregation during Lent will become a natural and welcome part of the life of the church during the rest of the year, and hopefully too it will extend beyond the confines of the church itself into the world. St Paul bids us welcome one another as God in Christ has welcomed us – the truth is that he has welcomed us with the open arms of the cross, and this is the sign of what it ought to be like among us. If we will not love someone whom we have seen, then we cannot possibly love the God whom we have never seen (1 John 4:20). The Lord's command is plain and direct – Love one another as I have loved you: abide in my love.

It is this abiding in the love of the Lord which bind the themes of martyrdom together. For it is the same deep trust in God and in his purposes, which together enables those who give themselves to a martyr's death, as well as those who give themselves to a martyr's life, to go on with that which has taken all their strength. Life so gloriously given for the Lord's sake must merit our honour and thanksgiving; martyrs are deservedly on the Church's roll of honour as their passage from death to life is commemorated by those of us who derive encouragement ourselves to live with such singleness of purpose, to the praise and glory of God. For us the life of a martyr continues no less in the ordinary and everyday business of being the Church in the world, and in ourselves ensuring that the witness of the Church is bold and lively, and that it has about it that power to attract others, to seek after and find him whom we ourselves have found to be the way, the truth, indeed Life itself.

Questions for Discussion

1. What is the inspiration for us today in the lives of the martyrs?

2. Do you consider the word "militant" to be an appropriate description for the Church on earth?

3. Is it realistic for the Christian to live to the praise and glory of God amidst the pains and perplexities of life?

6

Transfiguration

It came as a very welcome change from the hot, heavy and humid atmosphere of Tiberius, to make our way up the Mount of Transfiguration. Delightful though the Sea of Galilee is, it is some three hundred feet or so below sea level, and it is a great relief when a journey takes you some considerable height to the fresher and clearer air. It was a somewhat hazardous journey up Mt Tabor: so far by bus, and then, after a good deal of noise and bartering, with the camels standing idly and haughtily by, a fast and dangerous journey by private taxi, which skidded its way to the top on a narrow and precarious dirt track. I hardly dared to contemplate the thought of the return journey downwards! At last we were there, at the top of the Mount of Transfiguration, and it was possible, after getting right away from everyone else, to sit and look and take stock – first of all at the quite magnificent, if somewhat hazy, view, which opened out for miles around. After the sultriness of the lakeside, the comparative freshness of the air brought that exhilaration which comes to anyone who, after the clambering and climbing on the journey upwards, finally reaches a certain stage and takes a pause.

There is a good deal in the gospel narratives about Jesus going up into the mountains and out onto the hillsides. Then, as now, the townships around lakes like Capernaum and Magdala must have been intensely noisy, crowded and busy. The mountain sides provided a natural and ready made place for silence, for reflection and for refreshment. It doesn't much matter, I think, whether this is the actual mount of Transfiguration, or whether it was a nearby hillside or mountain – to worry about this would be to miss the whole point of the narrative. My mind began to turn on the narrative of the Transfiguration as it is told us in the gospels, a narrative which now finds a place in the theme for the Lenten readings of the churches.

As with any similar hillside experience, it is the silence of the place which strikes you first. You can almost hear it as you settle down and take in the view. At once there is a hint here for all of us who have set out upon the Christian pilgrimage. We need regular staging posts, points at which it is possible to turn aside from the way and look, listen and take stock. This may take the form of a quiet day, it may lead us into a weekend retreat or even a week-long retreat. The need for such opportunities can be self-evident, not least in contemporary life where we have hardly any time at all to catch up with ourselves. It is a sign of the times that the retreat movement has become so popular, that places in the guest houses of our religious communities are in great demand from a whole variety of people who basically require space and some silence. When we have re-established our inner selves and we are ready for the next leg of the journey, we can set out more confidently.

Whilst it may appear at first sight that the narrative of the Transfiguration has little to offer us in the context of our daily lives, with its focus on the glory and the splendour of the transfigured Lord "his raiment gleaming white as the light . . . ", it is worth remembering that the whole event is overlaid with the shadow of Christ's suffering and death to be accomplished in Jerusalem. Thus it has everything to say to us. One of the antiphons of the Eastern Orthodox Church in fact reminds us that – "Before thy crucifixion, O Christ, the Mount became like unto the heavens, and a cloud was outspread like a canopy, while thou wast transfigured; there was Peter together with James and John, in as much as they deemed to be with thee at the time of thy betrayal also; that having beheld thy marvels, they might not be afrighted at thy sufferings . . . " So the splendour and the glory are inextricably bound up with the suffering and death of Jesus. For John the supreme moment of the manifestation of Christ's glory is his death upon the cross. Here indeed is Transfiguration, a veritable showing of

God's triumph and splendour in the death of the Saviour, in apparent abandonment and failure. But this Jesus God raised from the dead and brought to glory.

It has to be admitted that the account of the Transfiguration of Jesus is not the easiest to come to grips with for those who, like me, are always asking the straightforward question – "What is this saying to me for and about my life today? What is there in this narrative for me in the ordinariness of today and tomorrow and the other days of this week?" It has been argued that the Transfiguration accounts are entirely misplaced, that they belong to the post-resurrection narratives of the Lord's appearance to his disciples, and indeed that so much theological truth is embedded in them that it is difficult to get to the core of what really they are saying, both as events and in their meaning. Yet in spite of this I believe that the narratives are saying something which is both profound and important for every Christian believer. I am encouraged in this belief by a comment of F.D. Maurice when he writes, "the transfiguration . . . has lived on through the ages and shed its light upon all ages . . . in the light of that countenance which altered, of that raiment which was white and glistening, all human countenances have acquired a brightness, all common things have been transfigured".

It is precisely this last reference to the Transfiguration of all common things to which I would like to draw your attention. It is extremely difficult to understand; it lies at the heart of the problem with the passage. Ponder for a moment the context of the account of the Transfiguration in the gospels – it is not different in its presentation or introduction from any other aspects of our Lord's activities. It happens that "after eight days" Jesus, taking with him Peter, James and John, goes up into the mountain to pray. It certainly isn't the very first time he has done this, nor will it be the last. In other words, as he is pursuing something to which he is accustomed – the ordinary and unspectacular business of going out on to the hillside to pray – the glory breaks in and the light shines through. Moreover, it is at a stage in the ministry when the disciples are perhaps just beginning to realize that here is not quite the Messiah that they had been led to expect, and for whom they had been waiting, and who in Jesus they perceived to be the one. For it is at this juncture in each of the gospel narratives, either just before or just afterwards, that Jesus tells them that "the Son of Man is to be given up into the hands of wicked men – is to suffer, indeed is to die". How perplexed and confused the disciples were becoming; even more so as a result of the events on the mountain. But there was something about that experience which enabled them to persevere and continue in their following of Jesus. There had been a glimpse of glory: manifestly something had happened, something which it was difficult to describe precisely. They had been aware of his shining presence. Like those on the Emmaus road, their hearts had burned within them.

For many of us this could well ring true to our own experience. As we saw in Chapter 1, there are many who do claim a very real experience, a similar conversion experience of Jesus Christ – a glimpse of glory. In both their awareness of this reality to them and for them, and their subsequent testimonies to it, they are able to continue and grow in their faith. For those who may not experience "conversion" in the same way, but who nevertheless would claim a similar commitment and attachment to Christian discipleship, they may well also experience such glimpses of glory. These glimpses are not confined merely to these occasions; there are unexpected moments when our hearts do indeed burn within us, and an act of worship becomes the occasion of which we are able to say, "I have seen the Lord". Such a moment may come even as we're pushing through a crowded street, sitting quietly in our own front room, driving through a town – in such ordinary and everyday things, in these "common" experiences, the glory breaks in and breaks through. We weren't particularly looking for it, obviously seeking for a sign, feeling particularly pious or holy, but there Jesus was, or at least that's how it seemed to be – an intense "presence" of the Lord within and around, and in a way quite unlike anything that has gone before. The natural desire is to want to hold on, to grasp and keep for ourselves this deep inner assurance. And yet it is absent as soon as it is present – at least that's how it seems, and we must surely be content for it to be so. Indeed there are those Christians who never appear to have any such experiences and would strongly deny that their commitment was any less enthusiastic: rather, their experience is much more of searching and questioning, much more tentative and hesitant.

Whilst such glimpses of glory may be hesitant-ly experienced and indeed may not apparently be experienced at all, it is the common lot of most of us in life that major problems and difficulties lie ahead. There are the comparatively minor things which are on our minds, and about which we become preoccupied to the exclusion of almost all else. These concerns have a wearing down effect; if we are not careful they begin to take us over completely, to the exclusion of all else in our lives. Some comparatively minor difficulty has become of such disproportionate importance that all our wak-ing moments are taken up with this one thing. It can happen all too easily. Sometimes too our lives move in directions we had never expected them to, as a result of an occurrence which at the time seemed to be totally negative. Perhaps you are anxiously awaiting the result of an examination or a job inter-view – everything depends on it – and you fail. It seems that your life is in ruins around you and you are not sure which way to turn. Often when such things come our way, it becomes difficult indeed to see much further than the dark and depression which surrounds us. We can think of little that is positive or good. In the darkening of our hopes and the collapse of our lives (for that is how it feels) we begin to ask the questions – What is there in life for me? Is life really worth going on with? It is at such times of real despair and complete lack of any kind of confidence in oneself that it is all too easy to interpret all that has gone before, the whole experience of life thus far, in the same negative way. When I have talked with people who have reached this kind of crisis point and who seem to be caught up in this vortex of negativity with regard to themselves and their lives, it has been helpful for them to discover, given the altogether longer and wider perspective of life thus far, it has not always been or felt like this, that there remains still, even through their present darkness, some glimpse of glory, some element which has been affirmative both of life and self. Similarly, with the advantage of hindsight, what may at a certain point in our lives have seemed to us to have been disastrous, now, with the passage of time, has been revealed as a moment of new departure, a time for a fresh beginning. What was so negative and painful was in fact the point at which new movements began in our lives, change began to take place, and out of that utter confusion something positive and creative emerged: the birth pangs of a different way forward.

Here is the core of what is to be understood by Transfiguration. Here is the point at which God continues with us in our darkest and blackest moments and times; even in the turmoil of all that, he is quietly and gently sustaining us in our wretchedness, he transforms our weakness and inadequacy and failures into possibilities which we had never even thought of for ourselves, but which gradually begin to dawn on us as we face squarely the reality of our situation. In a sense this is the answer; so often we want to avoid or evade the problems and difficulties with which we find ourselves surrounded; they pile up on us if we avoid them. It is no use pretending that they are not there or that they will go away – they won't. Perhaps, we think to ourselves, if only I pray harder and longer, all will be well; and it isn't, because it is in the facing and the tackling and the working through of a particular problem or difficulty that prayer can be truly effective. To face the circumstances in which I find myself, to work through them in a realistic way, is to learn and discover something new about myself – and about my relationship with God.

I would not want to suggest that prayer is not an ingredient in this process, but we must not react to prayer as if it were some magical incantation which will be instantly effective! Our engagement in the process is essential. Yes, there will be also present, as in all prayer, an expectancy that God will be with us, that God will act, but so often our expectancy is that God will obey our commands or fulfil our own desires in presenting the solutions we ourselves have proposed, when he is quite capable of making his own conclusions and taking us forward in ways quite different from those which we had anticipated. We can be confident and expectant that God will act, but do not be surprised when your own plans and hopes for yourself are turned upside down.

There is of course that activity which is central to the life of the Church in every age, and which takes us to the very heart of the meaning of Transfiguration, and that is the Eucharistic celebration. It is here that in spite of what may seem to us in the West to be a desultory, confused liturgical tradition, the Eastern Orthodox Church in its celebration of the liturgy enables us both to understand and appreciate the Transfiguration in Christ as we pass from death to life in the sacramental celebration of that once for all event of Jesus's death and resurrection. Rather, the Eucharist is the occasion when, in the power of the Spirit, heaven and earth are one. We hear the distant triumph song of heaven, we join our songs of praise to those of the angels and archangels, together with the whole company of heaven, as together we are caught up into that unending hymn of praise: Holy, Holy, Holy, Lord God of power and might, Heaven and Earth are full of your Glory, Hosanna in the Highest. Here is glory indeed, the glory of heaven – the brightness of the Holy Mount, glimpsed and beheld as in Holy Communion the Lord of glory shares with us the blessings of the Divine life in the Bread of Life and the Cup of the New Covenant. The bread and wine which we have brought and laid before the Lord are in fact ourselves, all our life – "there you are on the paten; there you are in the chalice", wrote St Augustine – for in bringing the bread and the wine to the Lord's Table we are bringing ourselves just as we are, however it may be, individually as Christians, collectively as a Church and congregation. There's no distinction here, no one better than anyone else, no one more deserving; our basic human lives are brought and laid before him, just as the paralytic borne of the four was brought and laid at the feet of Jesus – it is time for the Lord to act. The Eucharistic Prayer recounts the wonderful deeds of God in creation and redemption, more especially in the redemptive work of his only Son. Through the life, death, resurrection and exaltation of Jesus our redemption and reconciliation have been effected. It is with the recital of this Great Prayer of Thanksgiving that this bread and this cup become for us the life-giving food of the Kingdom. That process which is the power of the Holy Spirit at work in the Church, and which has effected the transfiguration of the gifts of bread and wine, continues as the eucharistized, the thanked over bread and wine, is distributed and shared among the believers, so that the same process can be continued and effected within and among them as they feed upon this heavenly food by faith with thanksgiving. Nor should the process end there, for we are sent out into the world to love and serve the Lord. Holy Communion is not some kind of spiritual sedative or comforter, rather is it the very means by which we are strengthened and invigorated to continue the proclamation of the Good News in the world. "Send us out into the world to live and work to your praise and glory" are the words we pray together at the end of every Eucharist. It is not for ourselves and for our own needs that piously we come to receive Holy Communion. There will inevitably be this aspect to it, but in bringing ourselves – the whole of our lives – before the Lord in this way we come as a Christian community to represent our whole locality, the whole life of the neighbourhood or parish. And as such we go forth from the Lord's Table in order that we might continue the process of transfiguration out there in the streets and in the lives of those with whom we have to do, day by day and week by week – to be the leaven in the lump, the salt to the earth, a light in the world.

Transfiguration then lies at the heart of the Church's mission too as it goes out from worship, and in worshipping to proclaim the marvellous deeds of him who has called us out of darkness into his marvellous light. There are those lines of a hymn for the feast of the Transfiguration which come to mind at this point: "Since thou dost bid us leave the mount, come with us to the plain."

It would be fatally easy to "spiritualize" the Eucharistic celebration so that it had little or nothing to do with the reality of our lives, socially, physically, politically and so on. Nothing could be further from the truth. It is not a refuge from the things of the world but rather the port from which we set out into the world, the springboard for action. And the life of Christ, given and shared in the holy gifts of his body and blood, is to penetrate the manner of our lives in every aspect — body, mind and spirit. We cannot drive a wedge between the solemn and sacred act of that holy moment of receiving Communion and the way in which we order our lives, our priorities, the kind of life style that we adopt. As Mother Teresa of Calcutta is constantly reminding us, our commitment to Christ's presence in his holy sacrament is to be matched by an equal commitment to his presence in the least of all our brethren, in the poor, the sick, the outcast, the disadvantaged and so on. It is all too easy for those who hold a particular view of the Sacrament of the Eucharist to become so concerned about the manner of Christ's presence in the liturgy that he is removed to the almost exclusive confines of the sanctuary. That cannot surely be, and any exhortations to a greater frequency of Communion during Lent ought to be matched by a similar if not more vigorous exhortation to our being committed actively to the working out and working through of the facets of such Communions, in both a heightened awareness of and involvement in and with the lives of those in whom we perceive Christ to be – hungry or in prison or naked or in any kind of need. It is not a matter of either the spiritual or the social, in the Christian tradition concerning the Eucharist the two are different parts of the same celebration. The one without the other is bound to result in a distortion.

There are as well the more personal consequences of our being drawn into this turning from death to life, of our sharing on a regular basis in this celebration of Christ's passover and his invitation to freedom and new life in him. There are attitudes to be changed, attitudes to other people, attitudes to money, to life, attitudes to work; there are a whole range of decisions to be made and for which I need to take responsibility, at home, at work, over the way I order and shape my life. There is the way I relate to others, those I like and love and to whom I am attracted, as well as those I hate and find difficult or boring. At every point therefore the demands of the Gospel are to be wrestled with as they challenge me again and again to that transfiguration of body, mind and spirit upon which I entered when I took the risk and declared myself for Christ – I turn to Christ.

The Parish Communion has for the most part become the norm of Sunday worship within the Church of England, though whether that is right and desirable is open to debate. However, whilst for myself rejoicing and recognizing that this is so, and that the Great Thanksgiving has come to have so central a place in the worshipping life of our church, I must also sound a note of caution for it could so easily become a matter (perhaps in some cases has already done so) of familiarity breeding contempt. And this not only with regard to the actual celebration itself, the act of worship which can so often be lacking that deep sense of awe and wonder, the "otherness" of heaven, so intent are we on making sure that it is meaningful; but also and perhaps more importantly whether we have even begun to realize the very far reaching consequences that this celebration, right at the heart and centre of the church's life, must have for those of us who share this heavenly banquet, and the responsibility that is ours for becoming actively engaged in such a task: the loving of and caring for my neighbour as myself.

Questions for Discussion

1. Is the phrase "glimpse of glory" true to your experience of God's "presence"?

2. How is the Eucharist a sign of God's freedom and liberation for all people?

3. How far is the Church called to be a sign of protest in the world?

7

—✠—

Waiting for the Risen Christ

A long time ago now I spent just over a year as a priest student in Bucharest, attached to the Romanian Orthodox seminary. The one highlight which stood out beyond all else was the celebration of Easter. Large numbers of people had gathered around the patriarchate area outside the Cathedral; as the time drew towards midnight the crowds had grown to enormous proportions. The square outside the Cathedral (and the meeting place of the Grand National Assembly, with its guards looking on somewhat defensively) was packed tight with people of all ages. There were low murmurs here and there as they greeted one another, but the general air of quiet and silence was amazing considering the size of this vast throng. It was an excited silence; you could feel the anticipation and expectation which rose to a climax at midnight, when from within the dark and empty church, a symbol of the empty tomb, the Patriarch emerged in shining gold and white vestments, holding aloft a lighted torch on fire for all to see. His announcement was bold and direct, an announcement that all had been waiting for, some for a very long time and after a very long journey on foot, "**Christ is Risen!**" The roar of the response was – **He is Risen Indeed!** This burst forth spontaneously from the crowd. Thereafter, the Good News of Christ's resurrection spread throughout the people as they greeted the folk around them. Candles were lit, and suddenly the hushed dark square became a place of celebration and light. Easter hymns were sung in chorus fashion, and the general air of festivity and rejoicing continued through the hours of the night. It continued too into the next day, and into the days of Easter-tide itself, as you heard in the bread shop, on the bus, in the barber's shop, at the corner of the street – no longer "Good Morning, Good Day, How are you?" but "**Christ is risen! He is risen indeed.**"

So the great news of Christ's resurrection burst forth into the darkness of that night, it burst forth too and invaded the lives and the streets and the shops, the ordinary and everyday things of this oppressive Communist society. It seemed as if nothing could stop the progress of the news. Here indeed, to pick up a theme from our last chapter, it seemed as if F.D. Maurice's words were literally coming true, for all common things were in the process of being transfigured. A change had taken place, and it was more than simply a change of mood, it was a change which went to the very heart of things. Lent had been long and it had been hard going. The days of fasting, in addition to the generally meagre and austere lifestyle all the year round, had made the five weeks or so seem like a lifetime. No eggs, no butter, no cheese, in addition to no meat, had made for a diet of beans and yet more beans, with, occasionally, other vegetables. But the perspective throughout had been Easter; and the fasting, combined with prayer, served as an encouragement to intensify that freedom which we celebrate in Christ not to conform to the things of this world but rather to be transformed by the renewing power of the Holy Spirit. So in a sense the waiting for Easter, the anticipation of celebrating in this particular yearly cycle, as in every yearly cycle, the triumph of Christ's resurrection, had been building up over the weeks of Lent. We have already noted that in the early Church that waiting and preparation had sometimes been over a very much longer period of time, for anything up to three years, of which the period of Lent marked the last lap, as it were.

The ceremonies of Easter Eve in the West, which have developed along somewhat different lines, nevertheless have at the centre the same basic proclamation – **Christ is Risen!** The Easter ceremonies, as they are sometimes called, are no longer acknowledged as somewhat strange and esoteric, but rather through the work of liturgical scholars in all the churches, the liturgical celebration of Easter has begun to find a place in the worshipping tradition of a large number of them. Forms of service have been offered by the Joint Liturgical Group, and more recently the Liturgical Commission of the Church of England has produced a great deal of material in Lent, Holy Week and Easter. The Roman Catholic Church continues with its liturgical ceremonies during Holy Week, as indeed do the Orthodox believers.

And the purpose of such services is not the introduction of ritual and ceremony for its own sake, but rather the engagement of the whole worshipping community in that once for all Passover effected by Jesus, which is focused in a particular way in living through with him and in him in these last few days. So we are with him as he shares the Last Supper with his friends; we are with him as he rises from the table and makes his way to Gethsemane; there we watch and wait and pray; we follow the events of his trial, scourging and crucifixion. And we await his joyful resurrection. The words and the movement, the shape and the structure, the music and the silence: all of which go to make up the public service, the liturgical celebration, all of this is brought together so that all who participate may be drawn more deeply and powerfully into the saving events which we commemorate and celebrate. But more than this, the fact that we celebrate these events, through word and sacrament, indicates that we are not simply witnessing another Passion play in church, but that by means of a liturgical celebration that salvation and reconciliation won by Christ is even now being effected in the hearts and lives of those participating. The whole Church is in the process of dying with Christ in his death and being raised to new life in his resurrection.

It is the acclamation of Christ who rises gloriously from the dead which makes for us an equally dramatic moment in the liturgy of Easter Eve in the West as in the East. The lighted Easter candle is introduced into a dark and waiting church with the words "Christ our Light". All present respond to this symbol of the risen and living Lord, with the words "Thanks be to God". In some places this is repeated three times, and where it is sung, on an ascending note – in order to highlight and give prominence to this announcement which is made with joy and boldness to the Church today. The darkness of the church interior is gradually made light as the light of Christ spreads out among the worshippers holding their own candles. And what a clear and unmistakable sign there is in this night, in the words of the Exultet, the hymn which accompanies the lighting of the Easter candle, that the night is indeed as clear as the day. Here we are able to experience for ourselves the difference that the light of Christ makes in a dark and fearful world. Here we celebrate in word and in action, in symbol and in sacrament, the fact that the light has overcome the darkness, that the powers of oppression and sin and death have been conquered, and that we, by adoption and grace, have become the children of him who is the light and hope of the world.

As we come now to the conclusion of this book we return to the point at which we began, namely that process whereby we as individuals are grafted into the fellowship of Christ's Church and take on for ourselves the responsibilities which follow from that decision, "I turn to Christ". I have attempted to show throughout the course of these chapters that there is the ever present need to "earth" this decision in every aspect of our lives. Further, there will be the quite natural desire and need to have the opportunity to reaffirm what I said and did on that occasion when I actually made my decision for Christ. We have seen that all too easily the initial enthusiasm can begin to wane, new problems and difficulties arise, deep questions present themselves, questions which I had never really thought of, which had never really occurred to me. Moreover, attempting to live out what is set before me in the Gospel is no easy task, and the whole business of engaging intelligently with Scripture may in itself have begun to make more questions than answers! Yet in spite of this I remain committed to the following of Christ, and the opportunity to renew that Decision along with and alongside all those who profess the same faith is to be welcomed. Traditionally this has been done at Easter, in the context of the ceremonies of Easter Eve. This is where the renewal of baptismal promises continues to take place in many churches and congregations. In a number of places this is done now also in the context of the Easter morning service, in conjunction with that part in the service where the Creed is normally recited. Of course there are other occasions and opportunities. Indeed, as Bishop I find that in visiting parishes for confirmation services I am often asked whether either a particular group or a particular individual or indeed the whole congregation can renew their vows as they share in and with those who are committing themselves in this way at confirmation. It may be that someone wishes to make a fresh act of commitment after a long period of real rejection of Jesus Christ; another person may simply have allowed their Christian commitment to drift, having become so immersed in the demands of job and family and life in general that they haven't had time for "religion" until something has prompted them into thinking again; yet another may have lapsed almost as soon as they had been confirmed – a whole range of people who come to rediscover the Christian faith in a wholly new and quite often different way and who seek some form of affirmation and opportunity publicly to stand up and be counted. And even for those of us who simply go on in a rather undramatic, perhaps even lukewarm kind of way in our discipleship, we also need the opportunity for renewal of our vows, if only to give us a fresh realization of where our priorities really lie, an incitement to be somewhat more businesslike and enthusiastic about our belonging to Christ and the renunciation of sin and evil.

Maybe this is the point at which a word or two should be said about this renunciation of sin and evil. For this is a key aspect of any response to the call of Christ from the very beginning. And here I make no apology for mentioning the practice of Sacramental Confession. The general adage in this regard in the Church of England is that all may, none must, some should! There are those who should indeed reflect carefully whether this should be an aspect of the Church's ministry which they may wish to explore more fully for themselves. Yes, surely we do make "confession" of our sins in a general way when the Christian congregation is gathered together for worship, and yet so often it is the experience of individuals that there remains a real need to articulate and verbalize some of the deep things that lie within – deliberately sinful thoughts, actions and words for which we know and recognize our responsibility and from which we feel the need to be released and delivered. And it is this personal sacramental ministry which is offered within the life of the

Church whereby the Lord's forgiveness and release is authoritatively pronounced by those ordained to do so. This doesn't mean that this is the only and exclusive way to forgiveness, but it is a means whereby the individual conscience may be quieted and the point at which the individual's conversion to Christ truly celebrated.

So often "confession" has been viewed in purely negative terms, as pandering to a sort of shopping list mentality of sin, which in fact gets in the way of real and authentic confession, overlaid as it is with the form and formula. And yet making a "confession" is or ought to be in the first place much more than a confession. It should be a blessing of God for his continued and steadfast loving kindness towards me, even though I have strayed into a far country and squandered myself and my goods and lost my way. Thus the context of my confession of sin is not an unhealthy concentration on and negativity about myself, drawing me down into greater introversion, indeed it is quite the opposite – it is primarily a celebration of enduring love of the Lord, an affirmation of his goodness and continuing care for and about me, even to the extent of allowing me that freedom to wander from him, only to find that even at the point of my most deliberate and wilful sinfulness he remains faithful, his arms remain open and already he is moving towards me to claim me for himself, just as I am. There are too those bad memories from the past which sometimes surface long after we thought they had been safely buried or put away. Maybe there are things which lurk within which are too painful or too shameful to mention, dark and shady aspects of myself which I deliberately keep away from the searing yet healing light of Jesus Christ, and from time to time there will be those things which nag away within and which I feel truly bad about but don't quite know how to handle and be rid of – an outburst of temper in the family, a deliberate snub, a downright lie and so on, all of which can be brought out for resolution and forgiveness. The context of Sacramental Confession provides the opportunity for such opening up and out of myself, the occasion when I can truly own my sins for what they are and know that as I get up and go forth I am able to go on my way rejoicing. That huge weight which bowed me down and got me down has been taken from me, and in those powerful words of absolution . . . "I absolve thee from all thy sin . . . go in peace, the Lord has put away your sins . . . " the burden is lifted and I rise up healed, restored, forgiven.

It goes without saying that such events in our lives are difficult and painful. It is not at all easy or straightforward to spill out the ways and occasions in which I know myself to have sinned and sinned grievously against God, neighbour and self. To continue to wallow in the slough of self-pity is not helpful either, and may in fact not only be prolonging but actually hindering that forgiveness freely offered by God in Christ through the ministry of his Church on earth. So often we are our own worst enemies in this regard, for even whilst we may be ready and willing to forgive even the most heinous sins of others, ready to assure them of the Lord's forgiveness towards them if they are prepared to repent of the evil that they have done, some of us find it infinitely more difficult ourselves really to believe what we preach – that with the Lord there is mercy and with him there is forgiveness even for me, sinner that I am! Furthermore, it is not a forgiveness which is begrudgingly or hestitatingly given, it is the oil and wine of divine love freely and generously squandered upon us even in our most lost estate. When we are down and out God doesn't give us a lecture, shake his fist at us and threaten that if we do that again . . . or turn his back on us until we have earned his attention. In no way; rather we experience the strong embrace of his love to help us up, set us back on our feet and point us once more in the right direction. Yes, it is almost too good to be true, and yet it is this truth which sets us free and which is what the proclamation of the Gospel is all about. No wonder the gospels speak of that rejoicing in heaven over the one sinner who repents, of the feasting and revelry as the prodigal returns.

Such a restoration and reconciliation, such forgiveness so generously bestowed, does not however imply that we may feel free to love God and do as we like, nor that we should sin the more so that grace might the more abound! Rather we are called upon to intensify our commitment to the putting off of that which, left to our selfish selves, we so easily and readily slip into, and to the putting on of the manner and way of life which is demanded of all who would take up their cross and follow Christ. If we are truly to grow in friendship with God, then we shall need to put our whole selves firmly to the task of enabling the life of his Spirit to take root and grow within, and that inward life will show on the outside those fruits of the Spirit, mentioned in the New Testament as evidences that the new life of Christ is indeed beginning to take hold and enable us to grow into the uniquely beautiful people that God intended us to be, each one of us fashioned in his own image and likeness. It is not a matter of rejecting who and what we are, but rather of discerning and affirming the God-given gifts, some more distinctive than others, some very different from others, but none the less each of equal value in his sight. If we were able to muster but half the energies we tend to allow to be dissipated in negatively aggressive ways in working at those qualities of kindness, gentleness, patience, long-suffering which we are all so bad at, then not only would we ourselves begin to experience transformation and change, but those around us would too.

As we saw at the very beginning of this book,

the days of Lent are the opportunity offered us year by year by the Church in order to renew our basic commitment to Christ and the extent to which our discipleship is grounded in our daily lives. Often enough Lent has been both perceived and expressed as almost wholly negative, as the five weeks in the Church's year when we are actually going to have a difficult time, and if we don't then Lent will not have been Lent! The concentration must be on the identifying and rooting out of all that which keeps us from a full-blooded living of the Gospel. Hopefully, I have attempted to direct our thoughts and reflections in a rather more positive direction, and whilst in no way abandoning what Lent has traditionally stood for in our churches, have been anxious to point out that there are many and varied opportunities when during these forty days and forty nights we can address ourselves to an achievable goal.

The whole point of any framework or rule we might set out for ourselves, or indeed of any shape or form of discipline, cannot be viewed as an end in itself – because this is the thing to do in Lent, because this is what Lent is about. Lent is about nothing if it is not about the glory and rejoicing of Easter. The whole perspective from Ash Wednesday onwards is that we may become more like Christ in his death and in his resurrection. So it is in this, the final victory having been won, that we can go forward with confidence and enthusiasm not only during this particular season of the Church's year but throughout the whole of this year, through however many years God gives us to live our lives. And that brings us to the end, to that final and victorious reign of God when he will be all in all, and which St John the Divine sets before us so magnificently in the vision of the Book of Revelation.

Already that kingly reign has begun, God's Kingdom come; already we share in that joy and exaltation as we celebrate the inbreaking of "the end" in the here and now of our earthly existence. That process of gathering all things into Christ has been definitively and inevitably set in motion in the death and resurrection of Jesus, and it continues in the life of the Church in the celebration and proclamation of word and of sacrament, and in the faithfulness of lives lived to the praise and glory of God. This is the glorious hope of our calling; it ought to be an enterprise which fills us with enthusiasm and joy, but so often we make such a problem of it all! It is an enterprise too which basically is so simple and so straightforward, and yet which we in the churches appear to make so difficult and problematic. The whole matter both of Christian discipleship and of this book, which has attempted to point out ordinary, straightforward and realistic ways of living a Christian life in today's world, of that basic friendship with God, is well summed up in that well known prayer of St Richard of Chichester –

Lord Jesus Christ,
Friend and Brother,
May I know you more clearly,
Love you more dearly
And follow you more nearly,
Day by Day. Amen.

Questions for Discussion

1. What is meant by the words of the prayer "May we who share Christ's body live his risen life"?

2. Does Confirmation have a meaning and a value for today?

3. Ought the call to repentance and the way of reconciliation to have a higher profile in the life of the Church today?

Also available in Fount Paperbacks

The Mind of St Paul
WILLIAM BARCLAY

'There is a deceptive simplicity about this fine exposition of Pauline thought at once popular and deeply theological. The Hebrew and Greek backgrounds are described and all the main themes are lightly but fully treated.'   *The Yorkshire Post*

The Plain Man Looks at the Beatitudes
WILLIAM BARCLAY

'. . . the author's easy style should render it . . . valuable and acceptable to the ordinary reader.'   *Church Times*

The Plain Man Looks at the Lord's Prayer
WILLIAM BARCLAY

Professor Barclay shows how this prayer that Jesus gave to his disciples is at once a summary of Christian teaching and a pattern for all prayers.

The Plain Man's Guide to Ethics
WILLIAM BARCLAY

The author demonstrates beyond all possible doubt that the Ten Commandments are the most relevant document in the world today and are totally related to mankind's capacity to live and make sense of it all within a Christian context.

Ethics in a Permissive Society
WILLIAM BARCLAY

How do we as Christians deal with such problems as drug taking, the 'pill', alcohol, morality of all kinds, in a society whose members are often ignorant of the Church's teaching? Professor Barclay approaches a difficult and vexed question with his usual humanity and clarity, asking what Christ himself would say or do in our world today.

The Way of St Francis
Murray Bodo

". . . an exciting and convincing introduction to the saint who, more than any other, appeals to the twentieth-century imagination."

Church Times

Open To God
Brother Bernard

A study of the life of that favourite saint, St Francis, interwoven with the author's own personal story and a wise, joyful understanding of life today.

Walking in the Light
David Winter

". . . an easy-to-read version of St Augustine's spiritual biography, from which Christians throughout history have derived a great deal of help . . ."

Daily Telegraph

Also available in Fount Paperbacks

BOOKS BY DAVID KOSSOFF

Bible Stories

'To my mind there is no doubt that these stories make the Bible come alive. Mr Kossoff is a born storyteller. He has the gift of making the old stories new.'

William Barclay

The Book of Witnesses

'The little stories are fascinating in the warm humanity they reveal. Right from the first one the reader is enthralled . . . bringing the drama of the New Testament into our daily lives with truly shattering impact.'

Religious Book News

The Voices of Masada

'This is imaginative historical writing of the highest standard.'

Church Times

The Little Book of Sylvanus

Sylvanus, the quiet, observant man, tells his version of the events surrounding the 'carpenter preacher' of Nazareth, from the Crucifixion to Pentecost. A moving and unforgettable view of the gospel story, and a sequel to *The Book of Witnesses*.

Fount Paperbacks

Fount is one of the leading paperback publishers of religious books and below are some of its recent titles.

- ☐ THROUGH SEASONS OF THE HEART
  John Powell   £4.95
- ☐ WORDS OF LIFE FROM JOHN THE BELOVED
  Frances Hogan   £2.95
- ☐ MEISTER ECKHART Ursula Fleming   £2.95
- ☐ CHASING THE WILD GOOSE Ron Ferguson   £2.95
- ☐ A GOOD HARVEST Rita Snowden   £2.50
- ☐ UNFINISHED ENCOUNTER Bob Whyte   £5.95
- ☐ FIRST STEPS IN PRAYER Jean-Marie Lustiger   £2.95
- ☐ IF THIS IS TREASON Allan Boesak   £2.95
- ☐ RECLAIMING THE CHURCH Robin Greenwood   £2.95
- ☐ GOD WITHIN US John Wijngaards   £2.95
- ☐ GOD'S WORLD Trevor Huddleston   £2.95
- ☐ A CALL TO WITNESS Oliver McTernan   £2.95
- ☐ GOODNIGHT LORD Georgette Butcher   £2.95
- ☐ FOR GOD'S SAKE Donald Reeves   £3.50
- ☐ GROWING OLDER Una Kroll   £2.95
- ☐ THROUGH THE YEAR WITH FRANCIS OF ASSISI
  Murray Bodo   £2.95

All Fount Paperbacks are available at your bookshop or newsagent, or they can be ordered by post from Fount Paperbacks, Cash Sales Department, G.P.O. Box 29, Douglas, Isle of Man. Please send purchase price plus 22p per book, maximum postage £3. Customers outside the UK send purchase price, plus 22p per book. Cheque, postal order or money order. No currency.

NAME (Block letters) _____

ADDRESS_____

_____

_____

While every effort is made to keep prices low, it is sometimes necessary to increase them at short notice. Fount Paperbacks reserve the right to show new retail prices on covers which may differ from those previously advertised in the text or elsewhere.